The Fairy Tale Revisited

NEW CONNECTIONS
Studies in Interdisciplinarity

Shirley Paolini
General Editor

Vol. 9

PETER LANG
New York • Washington, DC/Baltimore • San Francisco
Bern • Frankfurt am Main • Berlin • Vienna • Paris

Katia Canton

The Fairy Tale Revisited

A Survey of the Evolution of the Tales, from Classical Literary Interpretations to Innovative Contemporary Dance-theater Productions

PETER LANG
New York • Washington, DC/Baltimore • San Francisco
Bern • Frankfurt am Main • Berlin • Vienna • Paris

Library of Congress Cataloging-in-Publication Data

Canton, Katia.
    The fairy tale revisited: a survey of the evolution of the tales, from
classical literary interpretations to innovative contemporary dance-theater
productions / Katia Canton.
        p.   cm. — (New connections; vol. 9.)
    Includes bibliographical references.
    1. Fairy tales—History and criticism.   2. Modern dance—Themes,
motives.   I. Title.   II. Series: New connections (New York, N. Y.: 1989);
vol. 9.
    GR550.C38   1994   398'.042—dc20   93-27277
    ISBN 0-8204-2309-2   CIP
    ISSN 0891-0073

Die Deutsche Bibliothek-CIP-Einheitsaufnahme

Canton, Katia:
The fairy tale revisited: a survey of the evolution of the tales, from classical
literary interpretations to innovative contemporary dance theater productions /
Katia Canton. - New York; San Francisco; Bern; Baltimore; Frankfurt am
Main; Berlin; Wien; Paris: Lang, 1994
    (New connections; Vol. 9)
    ISBN 8204-2309-2
NE: GT

The paper in this book meets the guidelines for permanence and durability of
the Committee on Production Guidelines for Book Longevity of the
Council on Library Resources.

Table of Contents

Acknowledgments

I am greatly indebted to my dear parents, Roberto Tross Monteiro and Antonia Marisa Canton, and my sister Tania Canton Monteiro.

I also want to thank my committee chairperson, David W. Ecker, who together with my other advisors, Barbara Kirshemblatt-Gimblett and Robert Taylor, provided my with knowledge and encouragement.

Special thanks to Antoine Manologlou, from Companie Maguy Marin in Créteil, and to the Lyon Opera Ballet staff. Thanks to Pina Bausch, Tamar Kotoske, Maria Lakis and Mary Richter. Many thanks to my inspiring consultant, Cynthia Novack, as well as Irmie Jost, Rita Barros, Cynthia Carris and Graciela Magnoni. I am also indebted to this series editor, Shirley Paolini, as well as to Nona Reuter and Christine Marra, from Peter Lang, and to Dwayne Snype, from the Brooklyn Academy of Music. Without their imput this project would have been virtually impossible.

1

Once Upon A Story

Introduction

Fairy tales, despite conventional wisdom, are relatively recent written versions of folk tales of magic derived from ancient oral traditions. They began to be embodied in literary forms in Europe, particularly during the late seventeenth century. Fairy tales became very popular texts. One of the first fairy tale writers to shape the stories specifically to children was Charles Perrault, who, in 1697, published *Histoires ou contes du temps passé*.or *Histoires de Ma Mère L'Oye* (Mother Goose's Tales), followed in 1715 by *Peau d'ane* (Donkey Skin). In the nineteenth century, as part of a nationalist movement in Germany, fairy tales were elevated to the category of academic research. The *Kinder—und hausmärchen gesammelt durch die Brüder Grimm* (Nursery and Household tales Collected by the Brothers Grimm), published in seven different editions between 1812 and 1857 by Jacob and Wilhelm Grimm, aimed to give a new status to stories derived from the German people.

Although most fairy tales have been based on ancient oral folk material, they cannot be regarded as relics of the folk tradition. Fairy tales are not ageless, universal, or neutral as we are asked to believe (Zipes, *Art of Subversion*). Through the adaptations of oral stories into literary texts, these tales have been edited, rewritten and modified mirroring the zeitgeist of their authors' times. They are works created by specific authors, designed within particular sociohistorical and cultural contexts. Perrault wrote his tales according to the codes of the Louis XIV court, whereas the Grimms imprinted new bourgeois German values on their stories. This is why fairy tales should be reevaluated and seen as sociohistorical and aesthetic documents as well as as the result of personal creation.

Over the centuries, fairy tales became not only prototypical literary stories, but also exemplary choreographic themes for classical ballets. Paralleling the translation of oral into literary texts, the transposition of literary texts into dance pieces also responded to sociohistorical and aesthetic conditions. Dance fairy tales are particularly associated with late nineteenth century czarist Russia, where the French ballet master Marius Petipa began to create monumental pieces for the aristocracy, based upon fairy tales. His classical works include *Sleeping Beauty* (1890), *The Nutcracker* (together with his assistent Lev Ivanov; 1892), possibly *Cinderella* (with Cecchetti and Ivanov; 1893), *Bluebeard* (1892) and *The Magic Mirror* (1903).

In fact, ballet has always been associated with fairy tales. This association began to take shape with romantic ballet's attraction to the otherworldly and the magical and the establishment of the ethereal ideal of the ballerina. This ideal was perfectly embodied by the transparent grace of Marie Taglioni in *La Sylphide* (1832) and culminated with Carlotta Grissi's combination of feminine charms and physical daring in *Giselle* (1841). The latter work, considered the supreme achievement of the romantic era is a tragic ballet written by Theophile Gautier, who based his story on a book by Heinrich Heine about the German legends of the Willis, ghostly maidens who danced to death any man they found (Clarke and Crisp 155).

At the end of the nineteenth century, ballet became increasingly focused on the formal aspects of the act of dancing, such as the technical virtuosity of the performers and the design of shapes and lines of the *corps-de-ballet*, which refers to the group of dancers who frame the scenes around the principal dancers with sections of pure dancing. During that period, supernatural subjects were still popular but it was fairy tale heroes and heroines who turned into ballet's exemplary protagonists, replacing the earlier vogue of otherworldly sylphs and dead nymphs. Fairy tales offered well-known librettos, permitting the choreographers to focus on the formal, spectacular aspects of dance. The stories' elements of fantasy, with their sudden changes in the narrative flow, were perfectly transposed into the virtuosic steps, jumps and turns provided by the balletic vocabulary.

A new development in the dance world has been the fairy tale's emergence beyond ballet's aesthetic canon. Fairy tales have reemerged in contemporary dance theater productions in various countries, especially since the late seventies and early eighties. In these new environments, the tales receive a totally different treatment, responding to the contemporary choreographers' own artistic and cultural values. These productions use fairy tales as choreographic sources in ways that rewrite, reinterpret, and therefore revitalize the meanings of the canonized stories.

Examples: in Germany, *tanztheater* (dance-theater) choreographer Pina Bausch created a unique *Bluebeard* (1977) and her contemporary Reinhild Hoffmann choreographed *Machandel* (The Juniper Tree, 1987), a collage of different fairy tales. In France, *danse nouvelle* (new dance) exponent Maguy Marin staged her own *Cinderella* (1985) for the Lyon Opera Ballet, while in England performance artist Peta Lilly re-conceptualized Peter Pan's tale with her *Wendy Darling, the Fairy Tale Becomes Adult* (1988). In the mid-eighties in the United States, a new generation of postmodern choreographers have consistently used fairy tales as themes for their dances: Arnie Zane invented his own version of *Peter and the Wolf* (1985), Ralph Lemon choreographed *Folktales* (1985), the group Kinematic developed a trilogy of fairy tale dances including *The Snow Queen* (1986), *The Handless Maiden* (1987) and *Broken Hill* (1988), and more recently, Mark Morris created his idiosynchratic version of *The Nutcracker*, which he called *The Hard Nut* (1991).

How are fairy tales presented and represented, from the oral tradition to literature, from literature to ballet and contemporary dance-theater? How do the shifts of medium change our perception of the tales' contents? How differently do the new avant-garde performance exponents present these old stories which have been canonized in children's collections? Finally, to what extent is the meaning of each of the new dance-theater fairy tales related to its choreographer's sociocultural background? Ultimately, which stories do these renewed fairy tale dances tell?

This book articulates these questions, discussing reinterpretations of fairy tales in relation to particular contexts within Western cultural tradition. The main purpose here is to question how literary fairy tales have become mythicized in Western civilization, considered neutral, universal, and atemporal stories, although they have embodied sociohistorical, political and cultural values related to their writers' or performers' own background and context. The idea is to examine the way fairy tales operate as cultural artifices or myths in their displacement within specific media and particular sociohistorical contexts.

The book particularly discusses the work and context of Charles Perrault in seventeenth-century France and that of the Grimm brothers in nineteenth-century Germany. Subsequently, it contrasts literary fairy tale versions created by these authors with Marius Petipa's use of fairy tales in classical ballet. Finally, it analyzes the appropriation of fairy tales by three contemporary choreographers. They have created pieces based on literary versions of classical fairy tales previously written by Perrault and/or the Grimms: *Cinderella* (1985), based on Perrault, was recreated by French *danse nouvelle* choreographer Maguy Marin; *Bluebeard* (1977), also based on Perrault, was restaged by German tanztheater choreographer Pina Bausch; and *The Handless Maiden* (1987), based on the Grimms, was reshaped by American postmodern dance group Kinematic.

The three works are examined to see how they translate the literary fairy tale narratives into the dance medium according to each choreographer's socio-historical and cultural background. Subsequently, an interpretation of the three productions discusses how these contemporary choreographers have reread the fairy tales and how these rereadings eventually offer new understanding of the meaning of fairy tales.

The book is divided into seven chapters. Each chapter discusses particular materials and is approached according to theoretical sources that support it. This first chapter introduces the research, delimiting its scope, discussing its significance, method and objectives.

Chapter two includes a sociohistorical analysis of the writing of fairy tale collections, focusing particularly on the contexts of Charles Perrault's late seventeenth-century France and the Brothers Grimm's nineteenth-century Germany. It surveys the socio-historical contexts of the tales' writers—from Perrault's validation of Louis XIV's court aesthetics, to the Brothers Grimm's enshrinement of Protestant bourgeois and nationalist ideals.

Chapter three provides a sociohistorical discussion of the Petipa era, particularly articulationg his production of *Sleeping Beauty* (1890), in relation to the codes and values of the nineteenth-century czarist court. The primary sources for this section include videotapes of Petipa fairy tale ballet productions, available at the Dance Collection of the New York Public Library at Lincoln Center in New York City. Other sources include the discussions of Petipa's ballets, his style and his background, as written by dance critics and historians.

Chapter four presents contemporary fairy tale dance-theater productions—Marin's *Cinderella*, Bausch's *Bluebeard* and Kinematic's *The Handless Maiden*—in light of a postmodernist attraction for nostalgia and convention, the failure of the myth of the avant-garde and the infatuation with meaning, after a period where abstraction was at the center of artistic concerns.

Chapters five, six and seven discuss the three dance-theater productions: *Cinderella* by Maguy Marin, *Bluebeard* by Pina Bausch and *The Handless Maiden* by Kinematic. Each of these chapters is subdivided in sections that are threefold: the choreographer's dance background in its cultural context; the presentation of the literary fairy tale source used by the choreographer, either by Perrault or the Grimms; a descriptive analysis of the dance-theater piece.

The first section makes use of dance history and theory to provide the choreographers' artistic background while placing them in the context of dance tradition in France, Germany, and the United States. The second section describes the narrative frames of the literary stories according to Propp's structuralist method. The last section looks at the performances by Bausch, Marin and Kinematic and articulates the choreographers' choices of movement, characterization, sets, costumes, lighting, props, and sound in relation to the narrative and meaning of the tales. It contrasts the aesthetic and sociohistorical values embedded in the contemporary dance versions of *Cinderella, Bluebeard* and *The Handless Maiden* with those embedded in the sources by Perrault and the Grimms. It also discusses previous versions of the tales according to folklore research by Alan Dundes, Jack Zipes, Max Luthi, Linda Dégh, Karen E. Rowe, Kay Stone, Ruth B. Bottingheimer, and others.

Many Tales, Many Dances

What is a fairy tale? There are many definitions for a fairy tale, each coming from a perspective of study such as Freudian, Jungian, Marxist, feminist and structuralist. Freudin researchers deal with indiviudal motifs of the tales, according to issues of sexual and social maturation. Jungian scholars explore cross-cultural significance of motifs, searching for achetypal representations. Marxists study the socializing uses of the texts, and feminist intrepreters focus on gender issues associated with fairy tale narratives. From a folklorist's point of view, folk and fairy tales may be studied, defined and classified according to types. The same basic types and motifs, such as animal helpers, the enchanted forest, the lecherous father, the magic tree, and so on, are found in stories from different countries in different times and numbered together under the same category. The most widely used system of tale classification is the AT (Aarne-Thompson), designed by Finnish scholar Antii Aarne (1867-1925) and later translated and enlarged by American folklorist Stith Thompson.

In the AT classification, the fairy tales or folktales of magic are listed from number 300 to 749 and are subdivided into tale groups that involve supernatural helpers, supernatural adversaries, superhuman or enchanted wife or husband, supernatural tasks, magic objects, supernatural powers or knowledge and others. Sometimes, the AT type index is cross-referenced with the KHM index, which refers to the tales of the Grimms' collection. For example, *Rapunzel*, which is classified as KHM 12 corresponds to AT 310 type, where it receives the title of *The maiden in the tower.*

Another relevant approach to the study of fairy tales is the structuralist one, established in the twenties by Russian scholar Vladimir Propp. In his influential *Morphology of the Folktale*, Propp has analyzed fairy tales both paradigmatically, delineating the functions present in all stories, and syntagmatically, studying different tales according to their particular morphological structures. Generally speaking, Propp defined fairy tales according to the arrangement of their functions, which develop from villainy or "a lack," through intermediate, variable functions and finally to marriage, or other functions employed as a *dénouement*. Terminal functions may also be a reward, a gain, the liquidation of misfortune or an escape from pursuit, and some of these functions may be absent and others repeated in each story (92-99).

According to the Proppian formula, the major task in the fairy tale is breaking away from home, replacing one's original family through marriage. Propp based his work upon a corpus of some one hundred tales from the Afanasyev collection of Russian fairy tales. Because these tales are international tale types with AT numbers, it is legitimate to infer that Propp's analysis would indeed apply to general tale types (Dundes, "The Psychoanalytic Study" 54). Propp's seminal work has been considered a model for the strucutral analysis of tales.

Because a structural, formalist approach gives insights into the stories' shape, I make use of Propp's classification of the narrative structures to introduce the literary fairy tale frames chosen by the choreographies: *Cinderella, Bluebeard,* and *The Maiden Without Hands.* Nevertheless, reliance on Propp's structural system is limited. It works mainly as an organizational tool, allowing for a systematic comparison between the literary source and the subsequent performance by each of the contemporary choreographers. As Zipes has commented, formalist approaches account in great part for the reason why we see the tales as ageless, universal, and eternal, as they tend to homogenize the significance of particular human and social acts (*Art of Subversion* 6).

The book uses sociohistorical, Marxist and feminist analysis to contextualize and discuss the meaning of the stories. Because most psychoanlytical analysis tends to generalize fairy tale narratives, disconsidering the importance of their particular verrsions, I have not made consistent use of it.

Each dance fairy tale production is compared to its literary source. The Perrault stories *Sleeping Beauty, Cinderella* and *Bluebeard*, used by Petipa, Marin and Bausch respectively, were taken from *The Classic Fairy Tales* (Opie and Opie) and the Grimms' *The Girl Without Hands* used by Kinematic were based on *The Complete Grimms' Fairy Tales* (Campbell, ed.). In order to compare changes or similarities in the content of the tales, attention is paid to the text as well as to movement, character development, sets, costumes, sound, lighting—all the theatrical elements are considered in relation to the narrative frame.

In dealing with literary fairy tales, I have chosen Perrault and the Grimms, as their tales offer important and representative examples of the genre. They have provided the literary sources for many of the contemporary reinterpretations of the "classical" fairy tale stories, from Walt Disney's filmic *Cinderella* and *Sleeping Beauty* to the productions by the dance-theater choreographers Marin, Bausch and Kinematic.

In speaking about the presence of fairy tales as thematic sources for dance, I use terms which define various movements and styles related to the history of the medium in the Western tradition. The term *dance* is used generically to embrace diverse theatrical manifestations in the field, from seventeenth-century ballet to contemporary dance-theater in various Western countries.

Ballet is a codified type of dance, which evolved from the aristocratic European *ballet-de-cour* (court dance) of the baroque era. The term *classical ballet* is usually given to a specific historical period and a style within the evolution of the medium in the Western world. It has been particularly identified with the work of French ballet master Marius Petipa. In the mid-nineteenth century, Petipa went to Russia to choreograph and direct the Saint Petersburg Imperial Theater and Maryinsky company. There he created ballets that are characteristically formalist, technique oriented and grandiose in scale.

Modern dance stands in contrast to and developed historically in reaction against ballet. It is identified in the history of Western theatrical dance mainly through the principles and practices of American and German choreographers since the turn of the century. Generally speaking, modern dance defended bare feet, and a more grounded relationship with the world, in opposition to ballet's ethereal qualities. Together with the dance, it emphasized a contemporary world view, privileged emotion over form and a search for both individual and universal expression (Anderson; Au; Cohen, S.J.; Cohen and Copeland; Fraleigh).

Tanztheater literally means dance-theater. The term was first used in its contemporary sense by Pina Bausch, who has led a whole new school of German dance. She was elected the director of Wuppertal Ballet in 1973 and changed its name to Wuppertal Tanztheater. Nevertheless, her ideas and style were coined from a variety of influences, which combined her training with choreographer and educator Kurt Jooss in Essen and her study of American modern dance during the sixties. *Tanztheater* is characterized by a search for an essential emotional expression, not centered in the movement itself, but rather in a combination of media—dancing, acting, singing, scenery designing—with no boundaries between them. It embodies a fragmented, collage-like narrative with subtexts that seem to be directly formulated from everyday experiences and then taken to extremes. *Tanztheater* performers substitute suits and dresses for leotards and other typical dance outfits and the musical scores often draw upon popular European songs from the 1930's and 1940's.

Postmodern dance refers to an aesthetic school of American dance developed in the sixties, notably by a generation of choreographers affiliated with the Judson Memorial Church in New York. Dance scholar Cynthia Novack identifies the characteristics of postmodern dance as the fascination with the formal qualities of movement, an "anti-illusionist" stance, a self-reflexive or ironic attitude on the part of the performer, a fragmentation or juxtaposition of styles, compositional devices

—such as the use of chance and the establishment of movement tasks—and narrative frameworks (228).

Postmodern dance is a term often related to the Judson Memorial Church group, consisting of choreographers such as Yvonne Rainer, David Gordon, Trisha Brown and others, who worked together in New York during the sixties. After an early interest of the Judson group with abstraction and "movement per se," these post-modern choreographers developed an interest in the fragmentation and the recombination of narrative. This can be seen in the work of Yvonne Rainer, especially since the early seventies, and Meredith Monk, who was not affiliated with the Judson group but who performed in their space.

The dance generation which has emerged in the eighties has increasingly reengaged in narration, resuscitating dance as a means of expressing content outside its own medium. But instead of simply focusing on the content of the stories they eventually tell, these new choreographers have also been preoccupied with the formal possibilities of storytelling, exploring the various potentials for structuring narrative onstage. That is how fairy tales reemerged as appropriate themes. They are pre-conceived, well-known tales allowing choreographers to play with the structure of their stories.

Postmodernism is a movement in art and architecture, as well as a current school of thought in cultural history and philosophy. In its basic principles, postmodernism is very different from post-modern dance. Postmodern dance in its initial phases was mainly associated with an analytical, non-theatrical and abstract dance language (Banes, *Terpsichore*), while postmodernism is often related to an allegorical attitude, a nostalgic historicity which includes the borrowing of past references, as well as, in art and architecture, a return to narrative, even if fragmented. In this research the concept of postmodernism will be referred to primarily for its nostalgic historicity and its obsession with the manipulation of conventions.

Danse nouvelle, in France, corresponds to American postmodern dance. Because France does not have a modern dance tradition prior to the seventies, *danse nouvelle* has mainly developed from the national theatrical tradition and foreign influences in dance. It coined from the abstraction of American dance, mostly through the works of Alvin Nikolais, Carolyn Carlson, Merce Cunningham and Trisha Brown, as well as the expressionistic trends of both German *tanztheater* and Japanese *butoh*. *Danse nouvelle* has come to embody a blended kind of narrative, where emotional content is the main source of choreography. Nevertheless, it is also carefully shaped through formalist *mise-en-scènes*.

The delimitation of the analysis of contemporary rereadings of fairy tales to three dance theater productions — Bausch's *Bluebeard*, Marin's *Cinderella* and Kinematic's *The Handless Maiden* — is justified by the fact that these works exemplify current international developments in choreography. The pieces are examples of different concepts, styles and traditions in dance in Germany, France and the United States, respectively, and their choreographers are the main representatives of these evolvements.

Pina Bausch is the founder and leading exponent of German *tanztheater*. *Bluebeard* is one of Bausch's most illuminating works and one of the first contemporary Western theatrical dances to use a fairy tale as its choreographic theme.

Maguy Marin is, together with Jean-Claude Gallota, Regine Chopinot and Dominique Bagouet (the latter just recently died of AIDS), one the main representatives of the eclectic *danse nouvelle* movement. Although it was commissioned for the Lyon Ballet and therefore choreographed with a balletic vocabulary, Marin's *Cinderella* reflects the aesthetic innovations of the new generation, particularly in its use of subtle irony and mixed media onstage. At the same time, it also invokes French dance tradition, with its balletic movement quality and its use of masks reminiscent of seventeenth century *ballet-de-cour*.

Kinematic is an American experimental dance-theater group, created in 1980 by Maria Lakis, Tamar Kotoske and Mary Richter. The group represents a recent approach to postmodern dance, as it employs indirect narrative, incorporating fragmentation, meta-commentary, collaged texts, and storytelling devices in its dances. Lakis, Kotoske and Richter, who themselves created, directed and performed their works,

have been preoccupied specifically with recreating fairy tales.
They created a fairy tale trilogy, which included *The Snow
Queen* (1986), based on Hans Christian Andersen's story; *The
Handless Maiden* (1987), adapted from the Grimms' *The Girl
Without Hands* and *Broken Hill* (1988), adapted from the
Grimms' *The Worn Out Dancing Shoes*. This study focuses par-
ticularly on *The Handless Maiden* (1977), as it is Kinematic's
most successful production and the one which most faithfully
exemplifies the group's choreographic style.

Since performance is an evanescent event, a detailed analysis of the dance productions is based on their videotaped versions. The book counted on the possibilities of recurrent
viewing of videotapes, which allowed for comparative views of
the material and attention to minutia.

The analysis of the ballet *Sleeping Beauty*, originally choreographed by Marius Petipa in 1890, was based on a 1983
videotaped version of a performance by the Kirov Ballet
Company (then, the Maryinsky company) recorded in Saint
Petersburg (then, Leningrad). The production was made
according to Petipa's choreography and Tchaikovsky's music.

Fairy Tales as Cultural Artifacts

This book is interdisciplinary because it deals with fairy tales
in different media such as literature, ballet, and dance-theater
and because it is based on theories coming from a variety of
disciplines such as folklore, critical theory, dance theory, literary criticism and philosophy. Another important aspect of this
study lies on the way it questions the Eurocentric canon of
fairy tales. The stories of *Cinderella, Sleeping Beauty, Little Red
Riding Hood*, as we know them, were embodied in Europe over
two hundred years ago and and still remain the universal, the
"classical" stories. But they are only particular versions of
these tale types that have been "mythicized" over the years.

The concept of mythicization comes from French author
Roland Barthes. In both *Mythologies*, written between 1954 and
1956 and *Image — Music — Text*, with essays from 1961 to 1972,
Barthes defines myth as a collective representation that is
socially determined and then inverted so as not to appear to

be a cultural artifact. Mythicization occurs whenever a certain object or event is emptied of its moral, cultural, social and aesthetic aspects and is thus presented as something "neutral" or "natural". What Barthes calls mythical inversion relates to the freezing of a sociohistorical event, which, therefore, loses its contextual implications.

Fairy tales fit the category of contemporary myths that have become ideologically mythicized, de-historicized and depoliticized to represent and maintain the interests of the dominant classes. This can appply either to the seventeenth-century French court of Perrault's time or to their contemporary use in the entertainment industry. Over the years, fairy tales were rewritten in household collections worldwide and turned into "classic" Walt Disney films. They have assumed different forms in publicity and TV commercials. In all these appearances, the fairy tales were presented as anonymous, universal, and atemporal texts.

Fairy tales have a history. Their different versions have authors, who in their turn, have created in response to social, political and cultural values of their context. In other words, the fairy tale has an ideology. And the "mythicization" process to which Barthes refers consists in the hiding of this very ideology. In *The Political Unconscious*, American critical theorist Fredric Jameson further ellaborates on the "mythicization" of the entertainment industry, where fairy tales fit via their presentation as anonymous literary collections. The author claims that it is within this category that ideologies are most dangerous because they are hidden, as they seem non-ideological and apolitical. Jameson sees narratives as cultural artifacts that need to be unmasked as socially symbolic and political acts (20).

Elaborating on Barthes's concept of mythicization, Jack Zipes defines the fairy tale as myth, as it "takes material that already has a signification and reworks it parasitically to make it more suitable for communication in an ideological mode that appears non-ideological" (*The Brothers Grimm*, 149). Zipes claims the need for the reinstallation of the sociohistorical, contextual settings of the tales and the creation of new versions for the stories which would propose alternatives to the institutionalized, "classical" versions.

One way to free fairy tales from their "mythicized" status is to restore the texts' historicity and allow for personal revisions and reinterpretations of the stories. This applies both to fresh, new reinterpretations of pre-existing tales in other media, and to the creation of new stories, for example in the Zipes edition of *Don't Bet on the Prince*, a collection of contemporary literary fairy tales. This book presents another alternative. It introduces the use of fairy tales by contemporary artists working in the field of dance-theater. They treat fairy tale themes as frames or conventions to be scrambled and reevaluated.

2

The Fairy Tales

From Oral Performance to Literature

Storytelling has accompanied the development of civilization in mutable ways, with tales changing their configuration and acquiring different meanings according to the peoples who told them. In "Magical Narratives," Fredric Jameson refers to storytelling as the supreme function of the human mind (*Political Unconscious*, 123).

The origins of the fairy tale in the Western civilization are in the folk tale of magic, a type of oral tale where stories were symbolically created and adjusted, according to the live interaction between storytellers and viewers/listeners. Within its oral form, the folk tale of magic is ancient, probably coinciding with the first communication rituals among human beings. Jameson alludes to folk tales as pre-individualistic narratives, where there was a constant interaction between teller and receiver; an interaction that even makes the different categories contradictory in themselves (124). While a lack of documentation makes it difficult to retrace the exact historical origins of the orally transmitted folk tales of magic, it is possible to study the formation of the literary fairy tale (Zipes, *Breaking the Magic Spell*).

The folk tale of magic is part of a pre-capitalist oral tradition expressing the lower classes' wishes to attain better living conditions, while the term *fairy tale* indicates the advent of a new literary form that appropriates elements of the folk to present values and behaviors of the aristocratic and bourgeois classes (Zipes 27). The oral world of the folk tale of magic is inhabited by kings, queens, soldiers and peasants and rarely contains elements of the bourgeoisie. Additionally, Jack Zipes notes that in their origins, folk tales were amoral and focused on real class struggle and competition for power, presenting a harsh reality of starvation, injustice and exploitation. He explains that acts of cannibalism, favouring of the first-born, the selling ans stealing of a bride, as well as the transformation of humans into animals or plants were all part of the social realities and beliefs or many primitive societies (6).

The reality of the lower classes in pre-capitalist societies was so brutal, it needed to be symbolically transformed in the stories. Thus, at least in the tales, the suffering peasants could become princes and princesses, get rich and perhaps live happily ever after (Weber; Zipes, *Art of Subversion*).

In contrast, fairy tales are literary products produced by the upper classes. They have been in existence as oral folk tales of magic for thousands of years but became what we call the literary fairy tales, particularly toward the end of the seventeenth century, when the French aristocracy and *haute bourgeoisie* turned them into a fashion while the printing industry allowed them to be propagated. Of course, this does not mean that folk tales of magic have vanished in their oral forms, as they continue to represent the cultures of many peoples around the world.

To the same extent that oral folk tales constantly change in their retellings, literary fairy tales have been embodied in different ways according to particular sociohistorical, cultural and aesthetic conditions. These conditions determined, for example, the institutionalization of the fairy tale as an aristocratic genre especially valuable for educating children as carried out by Charles Perrault in seventeenth-century France, as well as a monument of German folklore by the Brothers Grimm in nineteenth-century Germany. At the end of the nineteenth century in Russia, fairy tales became institutionalized as perfect themes for grandiose and virtuosic classical ballet pieces, choreographed by Marius Petipa as a mirror to the czar's power. Another context for the creation and reception of the fairy tale is twentieth century post-Depression America. The film adaptations by Walt Disney, beginning with *Snow White and the Seven Dwarfs* (1937) and continued by *Cin-*

derella (1951) and *Sleeping Beauty* (1959), embody a patriarchal, capitalist middle-class mentality (Zipes, *The Brothers Grimm* 24).

From its institutionalization in the seventeenth century, the fairy tale has remained a prototypical narrative in Western civilization. Although their frames remain, the values embedded in tales such as *Cinderella* or *Sleeping Beauty,* have been constantly remodeled, according to the publishing and film industry and the specific interests of the mass media.

Thus, in a TV commercial, Cinderella does not complain about the exploitation she suffers at home, as long as she can use the right product to wax the floor, which will facilitate her housework. And Disney's Sleeping Beauty accepts and awaits patiently for her fate of having to sleep one hundred years, singing in advance: "one day my prince will come."

The bourgeois appropriation of folk tales of magic started in the fourteenth and fifteenth centuries, when European writers like Geoffrey Chaucer, Giovanni Boccacio, and Gianfrancesco Straporola began transcribing orally transmitted stories, while priests and ministers incorporated them into their sermons and religious texts for the masses (Zipes, *The Brothers Grimm* 22). The stories were then considered vulgar and amoral and were changed and adapted to legitimize the status quo and propagate the virtues of order, discipline, cleanliness, industriousness (Zipes, *Breaking the Magic Spell* 12). In *Italian Folktales*, Italo Calvino explains that fairy tales appeared in manuscript forms in Italy as early as in the middle of the sixteenth century, long before any other European country (xv).

In *Folktales and Society*, Linda Dégh explains that in feudal societies, storytelling became a service expected from the serf to entertain and distract the reigning classes. At the same time the practice was socially marginalized as it was seen as belonging to the people. "While the folktale was the best-loved entertainment at ducal banquets and in the bedrooms of the big landowners, the tales circulating among the people were branded by both the clerical and the secular powers as damnable and inspired by the devil" (65-66).

In the sixteenth, seventeenth and eighteenth centuries, the folk tales of magic of the common people were increasingly appropriated and transformed by the aristocracy and bourgeoisie. With the expansion of printing and publishing techniques, a new literary genre developed. Folk motifs became particularly reflective of the morals of the French court of the late seventeenth century and were also turned into children's literature.

This happened at a time when French absolutism was setting standards of civilization for the rest of Europe (Zipes, *Art of Subversion* 9). In the court of Louis XIV, the fairy tale represented and legitimized the norms of absolutism and a French craze for fairy tales was created within aristocratic settings. Although Charles Perrault has remained the most popular author of that time, fairy tales then were written mainly by court ladies, such as Madame D'Aulnoy, Mademoiselle L'Heritier, Mademoiselle de Lubert, Madame de Beaumont, and Madame de Murat. Telling tales provided diversion and, for these female writers, they also presented a way to express discontentment with marital arrangements and patriarchal domination (Zipes, *The Brothers Grimm* 82).

Socially, *la mode des contes de fées* was spread among the court members of Louis XIV, who were engaged in refining the folk tales of magic that many have learned from their servants. The term *fairy tale* emanated from the French *contes de fées*, which was probably coined by court lady Countess D'Aulnoy's book *Contes de Fées*, published in 1698, a time when the French aristocracy was immersed in a craze of fairy tale writing and retelling.

The term *contes de fées* is, however, strangely innaccurate, since fairies are not necessarily found in the stories. The term was actually created to separate what belonged to the uneducated and peasant, from what was cultivated and aristocratic. Formulating a separate term, fairy tale, writers also established the distinction between what came directly from experience and social struggle, and what became a matter of fantasy.

Jack Zipes clarifies the distinction between folk tales of magic and literary fairy tales by highlighting of the social connotations of the historical origins of the terms. According to him, originally the symbolic magic of folk tales had a utopian, emancipatory function, as they were created, spread out orally and transformed by the common people to compensate for the injustices of their everyday lives. However, through their historical developments, folk tales of magic were appropriated by the aristocratic and bourgeois writers in the sixteenth, seventeenth and eighteenth centuries. With the expansion of publishing, orally transmitted tales of magic became a new literary genre—the fairy tale (Zipes, *Art of Subversion* 7).

Based on oral stories constantly reshaped in different historical epochs by the live interactions between narrators and audience, fairy tales became literary products available only for the rich and the few people who had access to reading. Although it occasionally criticized some aspects of the status quo, the overall content of the literary fairy tale subscribed to an ideology that functioned on behalf of the upper class (Zipes, *Breaking the Magic* 11-12). At the same time, as Brazilian scholar Joseph M. Luyten points out, whenever certain folk tales were chosen, appropriated and adapted by the upper classes, they were abandoned by the people who have been carrying on the oral tradition (23).

Not all fairy tales have derived from the oral folk tale. Recent scholarship has found that some of the literary fairy tales were not even based on folk tales of magic but invented by fairy tale writers. German scholar Rudolf Schenda argues against generalizing misconceptions which necessarily connect the fairy tale with lower class origins and orality (78-79). In his popular *The Uses of Enchantment*, Bruno Bettelheim affirms that the tale *Bluebeard*, for example, was invented by Charles Perrault and has no direct antecedents in folk tales of magic, although its central motif—the secret chamber which must not be entered and where previously killed women are preserved—can be found in some previous Russian and Scandinavian tales (299-303). This evidence confirms the fact that fairy tales are not universal, ageless and anonymous as we are told in household collections. They are rather personal products belonging to specific sociohistorical contexts.

Charles Perrault and the Lessons of Civilité

As Zipes has said in *The Brothers Grimm*, there is a certain nationalist quality to Perrault's fairy tale writings, "for his work is part of a dialogue about the possibilities of the French language and customs to assume a classical status equal to that of the Greeks" (102). During his incredibly long reign, lasting from 1643 to 1715, Louis XIV affected the lives and thoughts of the peoples of Europe to such an extent that this time of Western History is often named the Age of Louis XIV (Garraty and Gay 732). Louis XIV was the epitome of the divinely ordained monarch and through personal governing, especially after the death of Mazarin, he brought a cultural focus and a political leadership that Europe was lacking at the time.

The Sun King, the paradigm of absolutism in the Western world, became the generator of the values to be copied by all other European nations. Whoever wished to be considered civilized had to speak French and follow French fashions and manners; this was the only way to *civilité*.

The reign of Louis XIV was a time of grandiosities best represented in the cultural monolith of Versailles and its lavish gardens designed by Le Nôtre. It was also the age of an extraordinary cultural flourishing marked by the work of Descartes, Pascal, Corneille, Racine, Molière, La Fontaine, Perrault, Bousset and many others who shaped Western civilization deeply. It was also a time marked by France's expansionist wars against other European countries. France's wish of grandiosity as exemplified in Louis XIV's imperialist drives are an important factor in the fairy tale vogue of the end of the seventeenth century (Zipes, *Art of Subversion* 13-44).

Particularly in the 1690s, with the culmination of France's cultural predominance in Europe, the writing of fairy tales became a new social phenomenon as it related to Louis XIV's desire to make his court the most flamboyant and radiant of Europe. Although it became most popular in the literary medium, fairy tales were also produced in spectacular ballets and plays. One example is the production of Moliere and Corneille's *Psyché* (1671) which in itself influenced the subsequent development of the beauty-and the-beast motif in the work of Madame d'Aulnoy (Zipes, *Beauties* 4).

By the end of the seventeenth century, interest in fairy tales was strongly cultivated among courtly circles, including the king and his minister. French scholars Barchilon and Flinders tell us that in his youth Louis XIV would not go to sleep without having his valet tell him tales at bedtime. Minister Colbert, in his leisure hours would invite people to tell him fairy tales, especially stories like that of *Donkey Skin* (78). Long after his youth, Louis XIV was still listening to fairy tales. Gilbert Rouger tells of Madame Le Camus de Melsons who, in 1695, wrote a poem praising a woman who could entertain the king with storytelling (xxii).

In that same year, Perrault had already published the versified fairy tale *Peau D'Ane*, followed in 1696, by a prose edition of *The Sleeping Beauty*, published in the literary periodical *Mercure Galant*. Also in 1696, within the panorama of the fairy tale vogue in France, Mademoiselle L'Heritier, Perrault's niece, published *L'Adroite princesse ou les aventures de Finette* and Mademoiselle Catherine Bernard incorporated two fairy tales in her novel *Inés de Cordue*. One year later, together with the success of the 1697 collection *Les Histoires ou contes du temps passé*, containing eight prose fairy tales, two other volumes of fairy stories were published by Madame Catherine D'Alnouy, and a smaller collection by Mademoiselle Charlotte-Rose Caumont de la Force.

In addition, many fairy-tale plays were produced. In 1698, Paul-Francois Nodot published his *Histoire de Melusine* followed by Jean de Precharc's *Contes moins contes que les autres*, Madame Henriette-Julie de Murat's *Contes des fées*, Madame D Aulnoy's four volumes *Contes nouveaux ou les fées à la mode*, and other anonymous collections of fairy tales. As Jack Zipes says, within the next century, French high society was literally inundated with fairy tales (Zipes, *Art of Subversion* 14).

The sources of the majority of the literary fairy tales were French folk tales of magic, transmitted by nurses, governesses or servants and adapted by the aristocrats. But, as the French aristocratic society knew how to adopt and adapt the best of other cultures, it also coined its tales from the Italian literary tradition, through the writings of Giovanni Francesco Straporola (*Le piacevoli notti*, 1550) and Giambattista Basile (*Pentamerone*, 1634-6). Other sources were oriental fairy tales which began to be translated in France in the beginning of the eighteenth century. Part of the *Arabian Nights* was published in

1704 by Galland, and a collection of Persian tales, entitled *A Thousand and One Days* was published in 1707 by Petit de Lacroix (Zipes, *Subversion* 14-15).

The fashion for fairy tales of the late seventeenth century also indicate major behavioral shifts in Western civilization. Feudal manners began to be considered savage, natural behavior seen as barbaric and uncivilized. The *homme civilizé*, idealized by Louis XIV and the French court, behaved with intricate social manners, wore wigs and face powder and spoke in a baroque speech style (Ariés).

As Michel Foucault has demonstrated, the notion and practice of sexuality was also shifting (1978). Overt sexual behavior was curtailed, manners grew in importance, and the contrasting roles of men and women were sharply determined: men began to be seen as rational and active, whereas women were regarded as emotional and passive. In a patriarchal society ruled by a Christian absolutist regime, women were even seen as potentially subversive and some considered witches (Zipes, *Subversion* 33). Thus, practices such as drinking blood and corporeal sacrifices, which were part of ritualized experience documented in oral folk tales were banned and considered grotesque and outrageous in the European literary tradition. Sexual references were discarded or tamed.

Although Charles Perrault remains the best known author of the time, the fairy tale phenomenon of the seventeenth-century France was mainly embodied by women, courtly ladies who incorporated the telling of the stories at the salon teas. The folk tales to which they had been exposed as children, began to be reshaped according to the baroque, *précieux* fahions of the times. By the 1690's men began to participate in these games and what Zipes defines as the "salon fairy tale" craze began (*Beauties* 2-3). Both men and women would prepare and read their tales in salons and later polish them for publication.

The notion of *civilité* and its focus on good manners, refined speech and sexual repression paralleled and had a direct influence on the increasing concern with children, particularly in the upper classes. If before the sixteenth century, children were not seen as a category apart and were basically treated like small adults, by the seventeenth century they began to receive special attention. As French writer Philippe Aries has noted, the growing influence of Christianity uncovered that, like adults, children also had immortal souls. Special books, toys and new manners were developed to educate children and provide models of the perfect behavior. Although *la mode des contes de fées* included fairy tales for adults, many writers began to shape tales to specifically appeal to children. Then, literary fairy tales became useful vehicles for *civilité* as the stories' ideology prepared aristocratic children for their future social roles, guaranteeing the maintenance of the status quo. Charles Perrault was the first and main creator of fairy tales for children, although his tales were not exclusively concerning them.

Perrault was not originally an aristocrat but a bourgeois. Nevertheless, he was accepted and incorporated within aristocratic circles for a series of reasons. First, he was accepted because of his high education and intellectual background. Second, because, despite his bourgeois background, his values were similar to those of the aristocracy. At Louis XIV's time, the bourgeoisie was increasingly enriching and strengthening itself as a class. In order to legitimize itself, it adopted the values and manners dictated by the aristocracy.

Third and most important, Perrault endorsed Louis XIV's politics, including the monarch's military campaigns to place France at the center of the world. "Perrault supported the 'manifest destiny' of seventeenth century France not only as a public representative of the court, but privately in his family and was also one of the first writers of children's books who explicitly sought to 'colonize' the internal and external development of children in the mutual interests of a bourgeois-aristocratic elite" (Zipes, Subversion 20). He even dedicated his *Histoires ou contes du temps passé* to Elisabeth Charlotte d'Orleans, niece of Louis XIV (Opie and Opie 22-23).

Perrault's rise to positions of power was, in fact, less a matter of his own talents than a combination of circumstances that included family influence and diplomatic astutiness. Although he had been educated as a lawyer, in 1660 at age thirty-two, Perrault began a career as a "public poet," devoting himself to the glories of Louis XIV's reign, writing odes and allegorical works illustrating the monarch's achievements. This is how he became noticed by the critic Jean Chapelain, advisor to Louis XIV's most influential minister, Jean Baptiste Colbert. Following a fashion of the times, Perrault became a *préciosite* writer, writing embroidered and allegorical texts extolling the person, the glories and reign of Louis XIV. The allegorical prose-poem Perrault wrote in 1668, *Le Parnasse poussé a bout*, for the occasion of the 1668 war France won against the Spanish Netherlands, is the greatest example of that kind of writing (Barchilon, Flinders 36).

This literary propaganda added to the fact that his older brother Claude was an architect working for Louis XIV, led Colbert, the all powerful minister of finances and superintendent of royal buildings, to appoint Perrault as his personal secretary in 1663. Increasingly, Perrault became Colbert's *homme de confiance*, a situation that culminated with Perrault's induction in 1671, as member of the French Academy. Founded in 1635, by Cardinal Richelieu, the Academy was officially charged of producing a dictionary of the French language, moving toward the codification of thought and the imposition of structure upon creative expression, at the same time that Richelieu was accomplishing a centralization of political power (Morgan Zarucchi 3). The French Academy was the epitome of a social and intellectual status mirroring the values of royal despotism. In the position of an Academy member, besides other artistic and bureaucratic functions attributed to him, Perrault thus became enormously influential for an aristocracy where he did not belong.

Charles Perrault remained in the public service until the death of Colbert in 1693, when his name was then removed from the list of writers supported by the government. At that time, a widow at sixty five, Perrault was solely charged with the education of his three children, Charles-Samuel, Charles, and Pierre. His decision to write fairy tales was taken from the fashion of the times and his personal admiration for La Fontaine's fables, as well as because he envisioned them as an exemplary way to educate his own children.

One year later, in 1694, Perrault published *Peau D'Ane* (Donkey Skin), his first fairy tale, written in verse. Its immediate success made him plan a collection of various fairy tales, which he would put together under the fictional name *Ma mère L'Oyle* (Mother Goose). An invented figure of the oral folk tradition, Mother Goose is the prototypical French storyteller. In using her name, Perrault expressed a wish to tint his collection with a certain folk and thus legitimate tone (Barchilon and Flinders 90).

In the following year, after Perrault had written his *Contes de ma mère L'Oyle* in 1695, a separate edition of *Sleeping Beauty* appeared in the French journal *Mercure Galant*. The complete collection of *Histoires ou contes du temps passe* was finally published in 1697, containing eight prose tales which ended with a rhymed moral, including *Sleeping Beauty*.

Although Charles Perrault was the author of the collection, he signed it with the name of his younger son, Pierre, at that time aged eighteen. This happened in great part because of Perrault's engagement in the so-called "Quarrel of the Ancients and Moderns" where he defended the incorporation of folklore in literature, as opposed to Boileau and Racine's insistence on classical Greek literature. First, giving the authorship of the tales to Pierre, Charles Perrault could be safe against Boileau's literary accusations against his lack of refinement. Secondly, using the figure of his younger son, he could inject the stories with a typical naivete that would thus make them more appealing to children (Barchillon and Flinders 80-81). Perrault's main preoccupation was to transform his tales into lessons of *civilité*, at the same time that they could be attractive to children.

Civilité is the keyword to understand how Perrault's fairy tales were constructed to disseminate notions that would regulate children's behavior and homogenize their values. Perrault initiated this indoctrinating movement with the special interest of educating his own children. His intentions were to elevate folk tales to the category of "high art," stamping them with the imprint of literary *finesse* and with moral lessons which would playfully penetrate the minds of children.

The origins of the eight prose tales of Perrault's *Histories ou contes du temps passé*, can be found in motifs of the French folk tradition but mostly from literary works by Straporola, Basile and other French writers who had already adopted folk tale material and reshaped it. Perrault shifted again the narrative perspectives of theses tales, changing characters, settings and plots, so that they could fit the bourgeois-aristocratic civilizing notions.

The eight tales, written in prose, ended with one or more rhymed *moralités* summarizing the stories' messages in a stylish, refined manner. For example, the *moralité* at the end of *Sleeping Beauty* says:

> To wait so long,
> To want a man refined and strong,
> It is not at all uncommon.
> But: rare it is a hundred years to wait.
> Indeed there is no woman
> Today so patient for a mate.
>
> Our talent was meant to show
> That when marriage is deferred,
> It is no less blissful than those of which you've heard.
> Nothing's lost after a century or so.
> And yet, for lovers whose ardor
> Cannot be controlled and marry out of passion,
> I don't have the heart their act to deplore
> Or to preach a moral lesson (translated by Zipes 1991:51).

Unfortunately, Perrault's *moralités* have not been included in most of the English translations of his fairy tale collection. This omission prevents readers from uncovering important values and ideas concerning seventeenth century France, as well as the author's own sensibility.

For example, *Little Red Riding Hood* which was based on a French folk tale of magic, received a drastically different treatment by Charles Perrault. The folk tale originally retold the story of a little peasant girl who went to visit her grandmother carrying a basket of bread and butter. It talks about a werewolf who eats the grandmother, placing her blood in a bottle and her flesh in a bin. As the girl arrives, he dresses as the grandmother and tells her to throw her clothes into the fire. When the girl realizes she is actually going to be eaten by werewolf, the girl tricks him. She insists she has to relief herself outside. The werewolf thus consists but ties a rope around her leg. The girl goes outside, ties the rope around a tree and runs home.

Perrault kept the tale, but took out ritualistic passages which were part of the peasant tradition. For example, the ritual including drinking blood and eating flesh in the story actually indicated that the girl had acquired maturity to replace the grandmother. The brave and smart young peasant girl who is learning to defend herself against outside dangers is turned in Perrault's version into a naive red-capped bourgeois girl.

The focus of the story became the girl's disobeying her mother, who had told the girl not to stop to talk to anybody on her way to the grandmother's house. As a consequence of the girl's having talked to the wolf, she is guilty and thus punished: the wolf devours the grandmother and, after dressing like her, he ends by eating the girl too. The warning message here is clear: girls have to obey their parents and learn how to control their natural impulses. The *moralité* of the end explicitly warns girls against the danger of talking to strangers and being *coquette*:

> It is clear here that the young children
> Especially the young girls,
> Pretty, nice and well-educated,
> Should not answer to any kind of people that talk to them,
> It is not strange
> That a wolf would eat them
> I say a wolf, because not all wolfs
> Do exactly the same thing.

In a context of Christian patriarchal absolutism, women were at the center of Perrault's attention. Perrault's tales directed to women reflect the ideal of the *femme civilizé* who is required to be beautiful, docile, polite, passive, industrious, and know how to control herself.

Like *Little Red Riding Hood*, *Bluebeard* is a warning tale against women's curiosity and lack of self-control. The only difference is that in the latter, the woman is not killed because she realizes her error of having opened the forbidden cham-

ber and says her prayers. Even in this case, it is only with
men's help—the arrival of her brothers—that the woman's life
is saved. Another example of Perrault's tales directed to
women, *Cinderella* describes an industrious, sweet and self-
effacing woman, who only after dressing properly acquires the
prince's love.

Endorsing docile and naive passivity, Perrault is not only
responding to the values of the seventeenth- century French
aristocracy, but also to his own fears. As French scholar Liliane
Mourney explains (1978), when Perrault argues for the total
submission of the woman to her husband, he is fearing
coquetry. Feminine coquetry, the only privilege of aristocratic
woman, upsets him since it represents a symbol of female
power which could endanger the fundamental values of society: the couple and the family (Zipes, *Subversion* 25).

Perrault's male heroes are totally different from his passive
and pretty women. They are active, intelligent and civilized,
reflecting the *haute bourgeois* male accepted at the Louis XIV
court, perhaps like Perrault's own character. In *Ricky of the
Tuft*, for example, prince Ricky is ugly and deformed, but his
intelligence is extremely powerful. In the story, Ricky meets a
stupid beautiful princess who promises to marry him in a year
if he endows her with brains. After she enjoys her new brains
for a year, she wants to break her engagement, but Ricky's
ability lead her to believe that she now has the power to make
him appear handsome.

Perrault's tales advise women to learn how to control their
sexual urges and subordinate themselves to the reasonable
men who know best what is good for them. According to Zipes,
this was a useful lesson in a time when younger women of
bourgeois and aristocratic circles were constantly being forced
into marriages of convenience with elderly men who were not
always particularly appealing. He also points to the fact that
women had become equated with potential witchlike figures so
that the control of their alleged sexual powers of seduction
was linked by church and state to control of diabolical forces
(*Subversion* 34-35).

La mode des contes de fées declined with the outbreak of the
French revolution, when the interests of the upper class had to

confront those of the lower classes. Nevertheless, the vogue of the French fairy tale, which lasted from the end of the seventeenth to the end of the eighteenth century, was directly responsible for the blooming of the fairy tale in Europe and the Americas from the nineteenth centuries onward. The values and behavioral standards established by Perrault's tales have exerted and continue to exercise power on the way we read and interpret fairy tales today, either through the illustrated collections written for children, the filmic versions of Walt Disney, television advertisements or other uses by the mass media.

The Brothers Grimm: Nationalism and the New Bourgeoisie

The Grimms' *Kinder -und Hausmärchen* (Nursery and Household Tales) did not contain only the classical fairy tale, also called magic or wonder tale, but also fables, novellas, legends and other types of stories. It is the so-called *Small Edition*, including the fifty *Zaubermärchen* (magic fairy tales), that has become popularly reprinted over the years as the Grimms' fairy tale collections for children. The compilation, first published in 1825 with subsequent ten editions, the last completed in 1958, was made to attract a virtual middle-class audience and it included tales such as *Cinderella, Snow White, The Little Briar Rose (Sleeping Beauty), Little Red Riding Hood, The Frog King*. It is also in the *Small Edition* that we can more strongly identify the values and morals linked with the Protestant church—family, ethics, work and homeland—as well as patriarchal middle-class notions of sex and gender.

Until recently, it was commonly believed that to build their own collection, the Brothers Grimm compiled oral folk tales directly from the peasants and that they only refined some parts of the material whenever it was necessary, maintaining the integrity of the genuine sources as much as possible. Nevertheless, recent scholarship has demonstrated that this was not the case. The Grimms made many more changes that we have been made to believe.

In his *One Fairy Story Too Many* (1983), John Ellis has demonstrated how the Brothers Grimm wrongly presented their *Kinder -und Hausmärchen* as a monument of German folklore, and introduced themselves as collectors rather than writers. More than is the case with Charles Perrault's collection, which was never intended to be a document of folk tradition, the Grimms' collection has been profoundly mythicized, becoming one of the most powerful cultural conventions in the Western tradition.

Ellis's book tries to demythicize this convention, clarifying some misbeliefs regarding the "authenticity" of the Grimms' tales. The author makes detailed explanations of how the Brothers concealed the identity of their sources and informants, referring only to regions of the tales' origins, giving the impression that the folk of that region was the source. The only storyteller explicitly named as a source in the collection — the KHM was originally scholarly annotated — was Dorothea Viehmann, whom the Grimms claimed was an old German peasant woman, and who has become the prototype of the Grimms' informants.

Discoveries made in 1955, however, revealed that Viehmann was actually middle-class, literate, and of French Huguenot origin. In fact, recent research has shown that most of the Brothers' informants were middle-class and literate women, who had learned tales which had already undergone previous changes. Besides the bourgeois versions of its original storytellers, the KHM was reshaped in each of its seven editions. The Brothers — especially Wilhelm, who assumed charge of most revisions after 1819 — kept adding new morals and values and refining what he considered unappropriated (Ellis 96). Despite this evidence, anonymous reeditions of the Grimms' collection continue to present their tales as a product of the Brothers' wanderings in the country, gleaning tales from peasants, in order to reproduce them as faithfully as possible (Ellis 21).

The significance of the Grimms' Germanization of the fairy tale material provokes heated polemics among fairy tale scholars. In *The Brothers Grimm*, Jack Zipes discusses the intentions behind the KHM and, disagreeing with John Ellis, concludes that the Brothers' building of a German style of the fairy tale was an accomplishment rather than a "crime" (79). There is no doubt that the Grimms stressed the Germanic character of their tales. They had strong reasons to want to link their work with the "genuine," folk German culture. Just as Perrault used his tales as manuals for civilizing the aristocratic-haute bourgeois children, the Brothers wished their collection to become a paradigm of German folk culture.

Rather than writing specifically for children, the Grimms were initially guided by scholarly principles and a desire to rescue what remained of the German oral tradition. The title *Kinder -und Hausmärchen* suggests, in fact, a dual audience, as *kindermärchen* are children's tales and *hausmärchen* are adult household tales. Only at the time of the 1819 second edition were they concerned with refining the tales to suit them to children.

The way the Brothers altered the stories also demonstrates a desire to find a "German" way of writing fairy tales, which set itself apart from the French tradition. In contrast to Perrault's era, literacy was condemned and meant contamination in the Grimms context, as it was opposed to the pure, genuine German *Volk* spirit that the authors and their contemporaries tried to capture.

Although nationalism is central to the writing of the KHM, it is dangerous to overinterpret the Grimms' intentions or make generalizations about the Brothers' writings in relation to German culture. In his book, Ellis criticizes German scholar Louis Snyder's argument that the Brothers' narrative choices yield actual elements of the German character, which he summarizes: respect for order, belief in the desirability of obedience, subservience to authority, respect for the leader and the hero, veneration of courage and the military spirit, acceptance without protest of cruelty, violence and atrocity, fear of and hatred for the outsider, and virulent anti-Semitism (101-102). These kind of generalizations have imprinted the Grimms's tales with negative, nationalistic tones. During the period of National Socialism, for example, the Nazis exploited the fairy tale in an ideological way to explain the supremacy of the German people (Zipes, *The Brothers Grimm* 94).

There are indeed characteristics related to the German culture which are embedded in the KHM collection, but they have to be seen under a much larger and complex perspective. The Grimms' collection is a cultural and historical institution, with a past inflected by the seventeenth-century French tradition. It is a product shaped by socio-cultural values of the German nineteenth-century context, filtered through the visions of two men. It is also an artistic creation which respond to their authors' particular backgrounds, ingenuity and personal values.

The Grimms' own drives were nationalistic to the same extent that their work appealed to German nationalism at the time of its unification. And the fact that their work was accepted and revered as a pure folk document is intrinsically related to its historical circumstances. The Grimms' patriotic motives were rooted in an urgent need to legitimize their own culture.

Historical investigation gives clues about why the Germans cultivated a strong sense of cultural identity (Ellis 2-5). Between the thirteenth and the eighteenth century, the country went through a period of relative cultural poverty. There was no "German Renaissance," and until the first half of the eighteenth century, German literature copied French writers, notably Racine and Molière, as well as Italian and Spanish writers.

Many circumstances explain this phenomenon, the main one being Germany's late unification. Until the early nineteenth century, Germany was not a nation but a compound of different principalities. These principalities were suffering from economic turmoil, especially since the Thirty Years' War (1618-48), a war in which every European power took part but which was fought mostly on German territory. Linguistically, the Germans spoke many different dialects, which discouraged literary uniformity.

It was a sense of cultural inferiority and the wish to overcome it that shaped the mid-eighteenth century movement *Sturm und Drang* (Storm and Stress), which had Herder and the young Goethe among its participants. The movement rejected the French neoclassical aesthetics that were based on the notion of *civilité*, which eliminated everything coming from a folk and peasant tradition, considering it superstition, irrational and uncouth. The *Sturm and Drang*, on the contrary, claimed that the most important insights of a culture could only derive from its folk tradition. The movement only lasted ten years, from 1770 to 1780, but it was fundamental in the establishment of German culture. The Brothers Grimm were certainly influenced by its ideas.

After the *Sturm und Drang* was over, romanticism grew strong around 1795, bringing an even stronger sense of nationalism. After having felt inferior to the rest of Europe, German artistic culture rose in eminence. Germany became the nation of music, and the center of philosophical thought, with the influence of Hegel's ideas throughout the continent. It was partly in search of their own cultural identity that the Grimms devoted themselves first to the study of the German language — Jacob Grimm was one of the founders of philology as a scholarly discipline — and afterwards to the collection of folktales.

Another major force that was behind the Grimms' work was political humiliation. In 1807, the French emperor Jerome Bonaparte had invaded Kassel, where the Grimms lived. In 1813, the French left Kassel and were defeated throughout Europe, which left an even stronger nationalistic fervor shared by the Grimms. But the time the Brothers spent collecting and reshaping the tales was during the Napoleonic occupation, and their intention was to counteract the occupation, fostering a sense of cultural identity (Ellis 100).

Another, and perhaps more important, set of events that shaped the Grimms' work was their own personal background. In *The Brothers Grimm*, Jack Zipes investigates the personal side of the making of the KHM. Jacob and Whilehm's own story is in itself a fairy tale as the Brothers struggled throughout their lives on behalf of their own survival, that of their family, their country, turning adverse conditions into great achievements.

They were born to a middle-class family, the older of six brothers and they were fond of the country life, being familiar with farming, nature and the habits and superstitions of the peasants. They were also given a strict religious education in the Reform Calvinist Church and remained always faithful to its moral principles. Their father Philipp Grimm, who was a prosperous lawyer, died when Jacob was only eleven years old, and from that time on the two oldest boys assumed total responsibility for the house and the family.

With the financial help of a relative, Jacob and Wilhelm were sent to study in a prestigious *Lyzeum* high school in Kassel where they were inseparable and totally devoted to each other—they slept in the same bed and studied more than twelve hours a day, becoming the best students of the school. They kept their moral integrity even during difficult times when they were marginalized by their teachers and colleagues because of their inferior social status and financial deprivation. When applying for admission to the University of Mauburg, they underwent great humiliation as they were required special permission to be accepted and were not given financial aid because of their lack of social qualifications.

At the University, they finally succeeded in studying with Frederich Karl von Savigny, the founder of the historical school of law who based his research on the philological and historical aspects of law. Influenced by Savigny, the Brothers got deeply involved with the study of literature and the customs of the German people. By 1806, both Jacob and Wilhelm began systematically gathering tales and folk materials. Clemente Brentano, the Italian writer, had become a good friend, and had asked them to help him collect tales for a volume that he intended to publish.

In 1810, after many difficulties—from Wilhelm's asthma and weak heart, to their mother's death and harsh financial strains which had obliged Jacob to work as a personal librarian for Jerome Bonaparte in Kassel despite his aversion toward French rule—Jacob and Wilhelm finally published the results of their studies on German literature and civilization, including research on songs, ballads, tales and the first edition of their *Kinder- und Hausmärchen*.

The Napoleonic Wars and subsequent French rule were a great distress as well as a propeller of the Grimms' work, as they were deeply dedicated to the unification and the cultural strength of Germany. So was their need to compensate the early loss of their father. As Zipes explains, the personal and the political merge in the Grimms' work, as the quest to reconstitute German culture metaphorically reproduces the quest to compensate the paternal loss—reconstituting the old German tradition embodied the wish to ressurect the patriarchal authority (Zipes, *Subversion* 34).

The Brothers' search for a stable home and for order and cleanliness as a way to compensate their personal, familial struggles as well as the distress they felt over the French occupation are mirrored through the selection and treatment that they have given to the stories. The Grimms's selected tales exemplified customs and language belonging to different strata of the German population, yet their constant revisions and reeditions of the stories colored the narratives and the characters with principles that belong to a specific Protestant ethic and to their own personal sense of struggle.

As a general characteristic, all the Grimms' protagonists begin poor, deprived or wronged, and after many struggles they achieve their goals. They usually come from the peasant, artisan or mercantile class and at the end they acquire power and money, a wife or a husband, and constitute a new realm. As Zipes puts it, they finally build a new home away from the primal home, as very few return to their old homes after their adventures. They rather go on a quest and establish a new home (*The Brothers Grimm* 80-81).

In accordance to these ethics, the Grimms' collection has stamped the fairy tales with the imprints of male domination. Although they adapted oral tales mainly from female informants, the Brothers treated the stories in a way that reinforced Christian principles of male hegemony and patriarchy. Similarly to Perrault's, the Grimms'female protagonists are always making it clear that the most important characteristics of a woman are her patience, diligence, obedience, and that her best place is in the house. On the other hand, male characters are outspoken, bright and rational. This can been seem in most tales, from *Cinderella*, to *Snow White* or the *The Frog Prince*.

But, even if male and female protagonists show often opposing characteristics, both genders respond to an ideology that fits the codes both of Protestantism and of bourgeois enlightenment. All the characters' adventures are set by destiny, and success is only achieved with hard work, cunning and the communication of the protagonist with helpers. Survival and self-preservation takes precedence over feelings such as love and compassion. In short, the escape toward a new home is the main task that marks the narrative structures of most of the fairy tales in the Grimms' collection (*The Brothers Grimm* 67-68).

Besides the values embedded in the tales, it is the Brothers' ingenuous writing style that was responsible for the great success of KHM. They eliminated erotic and sexual elements that might have been offensive to middle-class morality, added Christian expressions and emphasized specific gender roles according to their patriarchal code. Finally, they endowed the tales with a folk and cozy flavor by the use of diminutives and quaint expressions, as a way to pay homage to the peasants' oral tradition (*The Brothers Grimm* 103).

John Ellis investigated the transformation of the Grimms' tales over the years, comparing different editions with a manuscript written in 1810 by the Brothers, but only recently discovered. The manuscript of *Snow White*, for example, retold the story of a woman who narcissistically wished that her daughter could be as beautiful as she was. However, when the beautiful child grew up, the woman grew terrified, discovering the daughter was a separate person, indeed a rival. Thus, the mother tried to destroy the daughter but was eventually destroyed by her.

The Brothers Grimm changed what they found an objectionable theme, transforming the mother into a witch stepmother. Their version annihilated the disturbing emotional ambivalence. In the 1857 edition, the woman who wished for a beautiful daughter and got her, was not the same woman who envied her beauty or who was destroyed at her wedding. The Grimms created a context where the mother died right after the girl was born and was substituted for a wicked stepmother (Ellis 74-75).

Although the Grimms had consulted *Histoires ou Contes du temps passe*, and their 1812 edition contained such stories as *Puss-In-Boots* and *Bluebeard*, they later discarded these tales which would be immediately associated with the French writer (Ellis 92). Although the archetype of the Grimms' version of

Cinderella must have been Perrault's *Cendrillon*, the Grimms reworked the story, adding violent facts to it. This style, which favoured a punishment for evil, marked the German story-telling tradition from then on.

While in Perrault's version, Cinderella pardons her two sisters for being rude with her, in the Grimms' story, the sisters are physically punished. At the end of the story, during Cinderella's wedding with the Prince, two birds come and eat the two sisters' eyes, making them totally blind.

Another characteristic which became associated with the Grimms' storytelling tradition was a symmetrical writing style. In *Cinderella*, the two sisters repeat the same words and actions when trying the shoe on: they cut part of their foot off to get into the slipper and walk in the direction of the prince, while two pigeons cry each time: "Turn and peep, turn and peep/There's blood within the shoe/The shoe is too small for her/The true bride waits for you." Short verses are often repeated over and over throughout the tales. In *Rapunzel*, the sorcerer calls out to climb the girl's long hair: "Rapunzel, Rapunzel, Let down your hair!". And in *Snow White*, the queen mother repeats to the magic mirror: "Mirror, of the wall, who's the fairest of us all? As Ellis has commented, the symmetrical motifs and repetitive patterns, together with violent images, were applied to other stories creating a stylistic approach that indeed became a predominant "voice" of the tales (82-83).

This "voice" was shaped throughout the seven editions, and in the last, 1957, edition the KHM had 211 tales. The motivations that underlined the revisions and enlargements, made largely by Wilhelm, seem to be most remarkably psychological. As Zipes has attested, for Whilhelm, who felt that all the editions after 1819 should be addressed mainly toward children, it was as though he were bent on regaining a lost childhood or paradise. And through his ability to build the appropriate childlike tone, he created a uniform fairy tale style that has become "classical" (*The Brothers Grimm* 78).

In short, although the Grimms' tales were personal versions of European stories, the Brothers did manage to "create" a German tradition that ended by surpassing Germany and becoming one of the most successful cultural monuments of Western civilization. By placing Charles Perrault and the Brothers Grimm into context, it is possible to understand how the fairy tale was shaped according to particular ideological values. With the appropriation of the fairy tale by the publishing, advertising and entertainment industries, the fairy tale has become mythicized. It has been dehistoricized and emptied of authorship, context and ideology. The fairy tale has become a myth as it was presented collectively and anonymously, and its historical, cultural, aesthetic and ideological features were turned into the "natural," which is to say they were neutralized. The fairy tale was appropriated and corrupted by the cultural industry to become ageless, universal, the common sense, the norm (Barthes, *Image—Music—Text* 165).

The mythicization process masks the motivations that led to the adaptation of fairy tales in different contexts over the years. Since its rise as a literary product in Europe, particularly in the seventeenth century, the fairy tale has embodied a continuous dialogue with past and present traditions. It is its own malleability that makes it a prototypical element of Western cultural heritage. It is its potential for constant transformations and utopian impulses that shapes the strength of fairy tale narratives.

The frames of the fairy tale stories have been constantly reshaped alongside sociohistorical changes. These reshapings have been embodied internationally and interdisciplinarily, as tales were written in different ways, retold in different languages, and performed under many circumstances. Whenever a new cultural product, be it a book, a ballet or a contemporary dance-theater piece, makes use of the fairy tale as a paradigm, it establishes a dialogue, although nonexclusive, with Charles Perrault and seventeenth-century France, and with the Brothers Grimm and nineteenth-century Germany.

3

Classical Ballet and the Fairy Tale

Once Upon a Pirouette

When Marius Petipa began working as ballet master at the Maryinsky Imperial Theater in Saint Petersburg, in 1862, ballet already had a history of at least two hundred years. According to convention, the birth of the theatrical ballet tradition in the Western world took place in 1681. As Marcle Michelle explains in *La Danse*, this year marks the premiere of the emblematic *Le Triomphe de L'Amour*, a ballet in twenty scenes choreographed by Pierre Beauchamp with music by Jean-Baptiste Lully, conceived under the auspices of King Louis XIV in France (25-31).

At that time, ballet was becoming an aristocratic arform, presenting a code that perfectly embodied the aesthetics of Louis XIV's court. Considering the complex earlier developments of ballet previous to 1681, however, its history should start to be traced historically in the early sixteenth century, when the French aristocracy began importing dancing masters from Italy, and ballet became a symbol of refinement and social status.

Besides training the local courtiers to perform graciously during court balls, ballet masters also wrote dance treatises and manuals which popularized dancing steps and established a codified vocabulary. Although dance was practiced as a royal divertissement and symbol of status, it gradually evolved into a system, incorporating *pirouettes*, *demi-pointes* and other virtuosic movements, which finally demanded of its practitioners a unified formal training (Cohen, S.J. 5-31). While the Italians created the role of the ballet master, with such distinguished representatives as Fabritio Caroso, Cesare Negri, Domenico Ferrara and Baltasarini di Belgiojoso (renamed Balthasar de Beaujoyeulx), it was the French who turned ballet into a technique, a profession, a *savoir faire*.

In 1661, Louis XIV had asked Beauchamp to establish a definitive codifying technique and a professional dancing style. The master then improved the system of the *en dehors* (turned out), which already had been created in social dances but became especially important in adapting choreography to the newly created Italian stage, with its arched proscenium and frontal audience. With this new stage design, the focus of choreography had to shift from the group movements delineating floor patterns which appealed to audiences seated above in the foyers of palace rooms. The new concern was with the virtuosic performance of the individual dancers. When he retired from performing in 1670, Louis XIV established a school for the training of dancers and, thus, the Paris Opera was created.

Ninety years later, in 1760, the choreographer Georges Noverre published the famous *Lettres sur la Danse et Les Ballets*, a treatise influenced by the Encyclopedia movement of the Enlightenment era, claiming dance as an art and an expression of nature. In saying so, Noverre definitively attested to the transformation of dance from a royal divertissement into an authentic artistic language form (Cohen, S.J. 57-64). This change was strongly felt in the professionalization of the dancers. Instead of being danced by court members seeking amusement, the new ballets were by that time increasingly performed by especially trained dancers. Dancers became famous for their unique physical and virtuosic qualities and ballet themes and roles were specially created to display their unique gifts.

After the death of Lully, it was Jean-Philippe Rameau who became the official composer for the Paris Opera. Rameau was one of the main artists responsible for liberating dancers from heavy, conventional clothes and for developing and improving the opera-ballets, an artform previously launched by Lully. His best well-known work, *Les Indes Galantes*, produced in 1735, consisted of loosely connected scenes—a prologue and four acts—depicting stylized oriental or Indian themes: "Le

Turc Genereux," "Les Incas du Perou," "Les Fleurs, Fête Persane" and "Les Sauvages," set in *savage* America. The success of the piece was due to Rameau's musical talents, the fashionably "exotic" theme, and the musical and choreographic style adapted to acclaimed professional dancers, such as Mr. Dupre, and Mlles. Sallé and Camargo. Each one of them required Rameau to create pieces for their favorite steps (Searle 21).

The number of performers who formed a ballet company had expanded at the time beyond the four men (later joined by the four women) with whom Lully had begun working at the Paris Opera. By Rameau's time, a company consisted of fourteen solo dancers and a corps de ballet of twenty six. A new form of pantomime ballet or *ballet d'action*, conceived by Noverre and focusing on expressive movement, later grew strong in popularity. This form evolved from Rameau's opera-ballets, which already had a concern with drama and expression; its narrative, however, was mostly embodied through music and not gestures.

During the eighteenth century, ballet began to spread outside France and Italy and, by the end of the century, it was firmly established in several other countries, notably in Russia. There, in Saint Petersburg, Empress Anna de Courtland, niece of the reformer Peter the Great, founded a State School of Dancing in 1735, importing many French and Italian dancers to work as performers and ballet masters (Searle; Raeff).

However, at that time, France remained the chief home of ballet, with spectacular full-length productions designed in three or four acts and lasting a whole evening (Searle 56). It was also in France that the romantic movement in dance began to take shape in the beginning of the nineteenth century. The movement reflected the sensibilities of much art at that epoch: values connected with escapism, a denial of the rational world, a sentimental turning to the otherworldly, as well as an attraction for the exotic and the "savage" (Fleming 359-381).

Within the universe of dance, the emergence of the romantic style produced a radical change in the way people performed and perceived ballet. New choreographic themes were established where the female dancer became the protagonist of magical, supernatural stories. Romanticism in ballet stamped the ballerina's image with an ethereal imprint.

This imprint was initially embodied in Marie Taglioni, who became the prototype of the romantic ballerina. In the 1820s, her father Filipo Taglioni had decided to create a ballet for her, embracing the vogue for the otherworldly. Fearing that his daughter was too skinny, long-limbed and pale, and lacked the bravado of other dancing stars, he composed for her the ballet *La Sylphide*, in which she played the title sylph. Presented for the first time in 1827 in Paris, the ballet tells the story of a suffering sylph who engages in an impossible love story with a Scottish man until, at the end, she dies by the magic powers of an old hag.

The ballet became an instant success, and it also deeply changed the developments of Western ballet. Marie Taglioni's fast and virtuosic footwork was so influential that, from then on, all other ballerinas had to be technically skilled at using pointe shoes the way she did. Thematically, *La Sylphide* opened the way to a different choreographic style. As dance critic Walter Terry has said, the piece ushered in a new era of the ballet, where themes derived from classical mythology, popular since the inception of ballet, began to be replaced by European legends of fantasy and romance. The roles included nymphs, sylphs, ghostly maidens and, ultimately, fairies (327).

Marius Petipa was born in Marseilles in 1818 in a family of dancers, directly influenced by the styles and ideas of romantic ballet. His father, the dancer Jean Antonie, was Marius's own teacher, and his older brother Lucien had been an idol of the Paris Opera during the romantic era. Marius made his adult debut at Brussel's Theatre de la Monnaie, in 1831, performing in Pierre Gardel's *La Dansomanie*. Seven years later, he went to Nantes where he began choreographing. Since the beginning of his choreographic career, Petipa demonstrated a taste for the grandiose and exuberant, something that he initially accomplished by combining French romanticism with virtuosic Spanish formats. This was exemplified in his early works such as *Carmen et son Torero*, *La Perle de Seville*, and *La Fleur de Grenade*. However, his goal was best achieved during his long

career as a ballet master at the Saint Petersburg Imperial Theater with the Maryinsky Ballet company.

Since its foundation in Saint Petersburg in 1735, the first
Russian school of dancing had been directed by a succession of
French dancers and ballet masters. Marius Petipa arrived
there in 1847 as a dancer to perform a repertory consisting of
romantic pieces such as *Giselle, Esmeralda, Catarina*, and *Le
Délire (ou L'Illusion) d'un Peintre*. Petipa was later hired to serve
as an assistant to the former star of the Paris Opera, Jules Perrot, who worked as ballet master in Saint Petersburg for twelve
years, beginning in 1848. Perrot had given Petipa an excellent
apprenticeship, allowing him to even compose some ballets,
divertissements, and dances for three operas.

Petipa finally succeeded Perrot in 1862. His extravagant
ballet, *The Daughter of the Pharaoh*, composed in that year, gave
him the official title of balletmaster and marked the beginning
of the first distinctive period of his creative work. Music
scholar Roland John Wiley quotes the classification used by
Sergei Khudekov in his *History of Dances* to characterize
Petipa's work. Khudekov divides it in two distinctive periods,
each one distinguished by specific subject matter. In the first,
which lasted until 1888, Petipa favoured subjects with dramatic content, with a unit of drama containing a beginning,
development, and a *dénouement*. In the second, inaugurated by
Sleeping Beauty in 1890, he turned almost exclusively to fairy-
tale subjects (Wiley 18).

Working for the St. Petersburg Imperial Theater and
Maryinsky Company, Petipa choreographed fifty-four ballets
which reshaped the traditional Russian repertory and even
created a new dancing style. As Searle said, Petipa not only
controled the destinies of Russian dance for over fifty years,
but was responsible for rasising the quality level of the
dancers, who were to become the finest in the world by the
end of the century (67-68). Petipa is known as the father of
Russian dance. Ironically, what is considered to be the
"Russian ballet style" was conceived by a French ballet master
trained in Brussels.

But although the panorama of dance in the late nineteenth-
century Russia is often referred to as the "Petipa era," its high

standards were not exclusively due to the talents of the ballet-master. The Maryinsky's fame resulted from a combination of elements including Petipa's collaborators (with the director and librettist, Ivan Alexandrovich Vsevolozhsky, and with out-standing composers, particularly Tchaikovsky), as well as the availability of money provided by the State.

Petipa received most of the Maryinsky's glories mainly because, at that time, the first law of ballet was that of the bal-letmaster's precedence (Wiley 1). Both the composer and the librettist were subordinated to the balletmaster, as his author-ity over them was sanctioned by law in the Imperial theaters (4). Of course, the main reason for this supremacy was that the balletmaster was the only one who could remember and have control over his own creations, tailoring them according to political needs of hiring for specific roles. And Petipa was per-fectly adapted to this situation, as he knew how to manipulate choreographic flexibility to suit his ballets to new dancers and to the wishes of the aristocratic audience.

At the time when Petipa was elected ballet master of the Maryinsky, Imperial Russia was undergoing great changes. Beginning in the late seventeenth century, the country began gradually substituting its Muscovite orientation for an increasing Europeanization. Since he took power in 1694, Peter the Great decided to transform Russia into a modern and unified State. He founded St. Petersburg in 1703, casting it as a model capital in the fashion of other Western European countries. Later, in 1762, when a coup d'etat promoted her accession to the throne, Catherine II allowed for a great cul-tural flourishing in the country, revitalizing the University of Moscow and encouraging the systematic use of teaching meth-ods based on the European Enlightenment.

Gradually, in its search of self-legitimation as a country, Russia began importing European ideals of luxury and beauty. Russian intellectuals began to get acquainted with the writings of John Locke, the ideas of Jean Jacques Rosseau, and later the German philosophy of *Naturpoesie*. New academies and schools were established, the number of printed books rose sharply and the country saw a delineation of its own intelligentsia (Raeff). The development of intellectual and cultural life also became possible by the freeing of aristocratic citizens from State tasks—the decree of February 18, 1762, for instance, freed the nobility from the obligation to serve the state.

While these changes "modernized" the country, they also established a contradiction in the core of Russian civilization, opposing the formation of an intelligentsia influenced by the standards of European Enlightenment with the arbitrary, personalized authority wielded by the agents of the czar. This contradiction showed to be deeply rooted in the intrinsic dynamic of imperialism and early forms of capitalism, the anachronistic survival of an autocratic regime, and the failure of the upper class to understand what was going on in terms of socio-economic innovations.

This contradiction was dramatically illustrated during the liberal, reform-oriented reign of Alexander II, who abolished serfdom in 1861. His apparently benevolent rule lacked firmness and cohesion and was finally ruined by a movement of radical nationalism. After the war in the Balkans, revolutionary nationalist and separatist agitation intensified and, with the formation of the People's Will (*Narodnaia Volia*) group, it turned toward political terrorism. The group condemned Alexander II to death and assassinated him on March 1, 1881.

The government of Alexander III and that of his son Nicholai II halted the progress of reform, and undid some of what had been achieved, introducing the counterreforms of 1880's and 1890's, as a way to refrain the country from the radical changes that were provoking economical and political crisis. Censorship and control over intellectual activity were added to the imposition of strict new regulations governing student life and activities. This change effectively halted the further development of civil society and limited public participation in political life.

Economically, the reigns of the two last czars did help to promote an industrial takeoff, but at the cost of exacerbating an agricultural crisis, due to an imbalance between industrializing areas and an archaic agrarian structure. Besides sporadic upheavals led by the peasants, the epoch also witnessed riots in the cities, led by the new, miserably poor industrial proletariat.

At the same time, the personal authority of the czar had decreased. The distance between the Emperor and the Russian society increased, and, although the people continued to see the czar as their benevolent father, this paternalistic view was continued only through force of habit, as there was no further visible, symbolic, or ritual confirmation of this "political myth." The educated classes, the urban proletariat and alien peoples lost whatever was left of their belief in the sovereign's paternalistic and benevolent role. The court itself became less open, less public. Receptions, ceremonies and public solemnities were henceforth regulated in such a way as to prevent contact between the people and their sovereign (Raeff 193-198).

Ballet was one of the few public places that continued to serve as a ritualistic environment for social gatherings, where various members of society such as aristocracy, bourgeoisie and students could still occasionally enjoy the paternalistic presence of the emperor. In its spatial arrangements, the balletic audience even reproduced the hierarchical distribution of Imperial Russian society—aristocrats would sit in the loges, guard officers in stalls and students in the furthests balconies (Wiley 11).

Although these gatherings included members of different parts of society, ballet was specifically designed for the aristocracy, which made up the vast majority of its public. According to Russian ballet historian Anatole Chujoy, the nineteen courts of St. Petersburg with their entourages could themselves have filled all the theaters for every performance. There was also a singular place for the newly rich bourgeoisie, which was significantly placed next to the aristocracy. Russian dancer and choreographer Ekaterina Vazem recalls that this class was made up of railway concessionaires, factory owners, directors of banks and stock companies whose interest was focused on displaying magnificent clothes and expensive ornaments. Thus, appreciation of the art of dancing had been replaced by an emphasis on money.

It was under the spell of the counterreform period that Petipa's fairy tale ballets became not only successful but also emblematic of that era. Petipa's grandiose, formally oriented balletic style reproduced the past values of the czarist court at an especially conservative time in the country.

Since 1735, ballet had been virtually the property of the czar and, as such, an aristocratic artifact. It neither echoed the economic crisis felt mostly by the middle-class, peasants and the new urban proletariat, nor the populist and disillusioned sentiments of writers like Tolstoy and Dostoyevsky. As Deborah Jowitt has pointed out, the ballets demanded by Ivan Vsevolojsky, the director of the Imperial Theater, emphasized pomp and diversion even more than had their predecessors (242).

In Imperial Russia under Alexander III, the response to the threatening and overwhelming social crisis was an emphasis on pomp, luxury and entertainment as a means of distraction. This policy became clearly delineated when Alexander III appointed Ivan Alexandrovich Vsevolozhsky Director of Imperial Theaters in 1883, a post that he filled for almost eighteen years. Vsevolozhsky was refined, aristocratic and above all, obsessed with French culture and ancient Greek civilization. In 1876 he had been assigned to the Russian consulate in Paris, and over the next five years he developed a love of French civilization and a taste for Parisian life. Besides his refinement, the director was extremely productive and influential. He completed at least 1,087 drawings of costumes for twenty-five productions (including 221 for *Sleeping Beauty* and *Nutcracker* alone) and more that were probably lost.

Vsevolozhsky's contribution to the creation of *Sleeping Beauty* was key to the ballet's identity, and, although no copies of the original libretto have survived, it is generally accepted that he was the one who wrote its text. He was also greatly responsible for the grandious atmosphere emanated by Petipa's late fairy tale ballets. Besides his participation in Petipa's best-known ballets such as *Sleeping Beauty*, *Nutcracker* and *Swan Lake*, Vsevolozhsky's fruitful relationship with the choreographer resulted in a number of other ballets which evoked France's golden age, including *L'Ordre du Roi*, *Les Ruses d'Amour* and, indirectly, *Sleeping Beauty* (Wiley 94).

As a director of the Imperial theaters, Vsevolozhsky's task was not simply to provide entertainment, but to act as a bene-

ficial influence on literature, mores, and national conscious-
ness, as well as to establish a school and to encourage a tradition. According to his principles, the Imperial theaters were
not commercial institutions and therefore must pursue high
educational ends. His demands were stamped with the
imprints of moralism and nationalism, which made the director search for a true and grandiose identity for Russian dancing. Thus, he was firmly opposed to the participation of foreign ballerinas in the company.

Paralleling the splendor and grandiosity of the Russian
courts, ballets like *Sleeping Beauty* or *The Nutcracker* are so large
in scale that they contain courts of their own. And they all
follow a basic structural formula, with each ballet being based
in a *grand pas d'action* with pantomimes performed by two to
five artists. After that, his ballets respect the traditional format,
composed by entrance, *adagio*, variations and *coda*.

Petipa's grand ballets—four or five-act, five-hour dramatic
spectacles, with plots augmented by mime and divertissements,
with crowded scenes and large *corps-de-ballet*—gave the dances
imperial proportions. The choreographer diagrammed these
virtuosic *corps-de-ballet*, which did not necessarily play roles in
the story, but translated a superhuman symmetry, with the
dancers echoing gestures in a balanced and unified mode.
Very simple poses in adagio, repeated by the whole *corps-de-
ballet* create a striking effect. In *Time and the Dancing Image*,
Deborah Jowitt quotes Russian critic Akim Volynsky, who in
response to Petipa's *Sleeping Beauty* wrote: "There are every-
where lines and figures which harmonize with one another
and create the impression of one line and one figure" (251).
Since the beginning of his career, spectacle was a staple of the
Petipa ballet, and at the same time, his work is astounding in
its simplicity. Each dance is built out of two elements: the
arabesque for moments of repose, and short runs on *pointe* for
movement around the stage.

The Prototype for the Fairy Tale Ballet: Sleeping Beauty

In the history of Russian ballet at the end of the nineteenth
century, the grandious style of Marius Petipa's choreography,

the luxurious taste of Vsevolozhsky and the refined musical creations of Tchaikovsky, all combined to produce a body of work where the European romantic ballet's principles and values—the professionalization of dancers, ethereal and otherworldly qualities attributed to the ballerina, technical virtuosity—evolved toward the purest classical language. This language attempted, in principle, to revive the nobility of the courts of Louis XIV in France. Vsevolozhsky wanted the ballet's *mise-en-scène* to reproduce the French baroque style and the music to revisit the spirit of Lully, Bach and Rameau (Wiley 105). As Lincoln Kirstein has written in *Four Centuries of Ballet*, the aim of *Sleeping Beauty* was to instruct, delight and metaphorically express instruments of aristocratic power. It should ensure that the Romanov court was as stable and powerful as the court where Charles Perrault belonged (174).

Sleeping Beauty is Petipa's most successful ballet as well as Perrault's most celebrated story. It was the first to appear in his *Histoires ou contes du temps passe* in 1697 after been published in a separated edition in the preceding year. Perrault's version was written with so much wit and baroque lyricism that it remains more popular than the nineteenth century Grimms' version of the tale, called *Dornrochen*, or *Little Briar-Rose*. The Grimms' version was based on that of the French writer, although they always refused to acknowledge this fact (Opie and Opie 102).

The idea for the ballet came to Vsevolozhsky as a perfect expression of the imperial connection to France's golden years as well as a good excuse for a luxurious and magical scenario. Nevertheless, his libretto is far from a perfect reproduction of Perrault's writings. The librettist modified some parts, omitted scenes and created new ones, as will be further analyzed in this study.

Generally speaking, the changes in the ballet are related both to the different medium chosen for the representation of the story—from literature to ballet—and to the different context in which the story was rewritten and performed—from seventeenth century France to nineteenth century Russia. Nevertheless, despite these differences, Vsevolozhsky/Petipa's version of *Sleeping Beauty* maintains a tone and a moral message that is identical to that of Perrault's.

In the ballet *Sleeping Beauty*, the outcome of the story is known already in the prologue, so the rest of the dance merely confirms the first scene. Thus, as Wiley has pointed out, the ballet lacks tension: in the prologue, the good fairy tames the spell of death and assures that the princess's life will not be taken when she pricks her finger.

The lack of tension is also felt in the music, as there is no overall melodic development in the work. The prologue and the first act, for example, are symmetrical, with Act I replacing the prologue with princes in place of fairies. Each act illuminates one situation in the story, and similarly the sense of stasis justify in the music a tableau-like approach to key. The succession of keys chosen by Tchaikovsky is logical and inevitable, and it lacks urgency. We are but vaguely conscious of the momentum underlying the activity of surface detail in a fairy-tale (Wiley 131). As Wiley said, detractors of the work called *Sleeping Beauty* a mere *ballet-féerie*, a genre in which visaul indulge is a compensation for weakness of plot and story. The production was certainly indulging, as it spent more than a quarter of the total annual budget of the entire production department of the Petersburg theaters. Nevertheless, the ballet goes much beyond the business of imperial entertainment (107).

Sleeping Beauty is an allegorical ballet, and its allegory is multilayered. First, the presentation of Aurora reproduces the life cycle, with each section of the ballet evoking infancy, youth, love and marriage, respectively. The name given by Vsevolovzhsky, Aurora, or dawn, has implications of rebirth and springtime. This aspect was already perceived by Russian critics such as Boris Asafiev at the time of its premiere (Wiley 108).

Another allegorical aspect of Petipa's ballets lies in their utilization of dancers to reproduce the composition and functioning of Russian society at that time. The ballet and opera state companies in Russia were constantly inflated in order to hire persons that the czar or his courtiers had to favor politically or personally. This fact is directly linked to Petipa's frequent use of a huge *corps-de-ballet* in each of his ballets, employing as many people as he could.

The hierarchical composition of the ballets, from *premier danseur* or *danseuse* to the *corps-de-ballet*, reproduced the arrangements and protocol of the Imperialist society. As Deborah Jowitt said, Petipa found essential that the choreographies mirrored Imperial values within their own structural organization (*Time and the Dancing Image*, 243).

The final allegory refers to *Sleeping Beauty*'s commentary on a specific time in Imperial Russia's political life. The librettist's choice to place the ballet during Louis XIV's time, substituting the figure of the Sun King for that of a fictional King Florestan, can be seen as a significant assessment of Alexander III's own reign, when the czar was losing popularity and control over the country (Wiley 149).

Although the ballet presented a style that reproduced the monarchic protocols, it was also created in a way that functioned as a subtle response to them, with his depiction of a king who commits a fault in royal courtesy and protocol — he forgets to invite the wicked fairy, and he will have to pay for it. Could Vsevolozhsky and Petipa be indicating the czar that he was doing something wrong in the way he was governing the country?

Narrative Structures

An understanding of the values imbedded in Petipa's *Sleeping Beauty* and the significance of its sociohistorical context require a comparative analysis with its literary source. A systematic way of comparing the ballet's narrative to Perrault's literary text can be adapted from Russian folklorist and structural analyst Vladimir Propp.

Borrowing from the concept of syntax in the study of language, Propp's syntagmatic system offers a formal narrative analysis of the text, following the chronological order of the sequence of elements in it. As Dundes said in his introduction of *Morphology of the Folktale*, this method identifies units for a comparison between the two versions of the tale and enables a subsequent paradigmatic study, in which the pattern that underlines the narrative is analyzed (ix-x).

The Aarne-Thompson index classifies the *Sleeping Beauty* tale variants as n. 410, while in the Brothers Grimms' classification, it appears as KHM n. 50. The ballet *Sleeping Beauty* is based on Perrault's version. But here it is not dancing itself that narrates the story; the tale is told primarily by mimed gestures and also by costumes, scenery and music. The elements that embody narrative are punctuated by almost pure, abstract dancing, with the *corps-de-ballet* performing symmetrical patterns, while individual dancers engage in *pas de deux, trois* or *quatre* displaying virtuosic arabesques, jumps or turns. There is thus a clear separation between narrative and the dancing per se, a procedure that can be seen in the sixteenth-seventeenth century *ballet a entrées*, as well as in most Hollywood musicals of the 1930s, where actors-dancers would stop the action to dance and vice-versa.

Segmenting the plot according to Propp's classification, it is possible to compare Perrault's *La belle au bois dormant* with Petipa's version of the story. Each section of the plot will be presented according to Perrault and, subsequently, to Petipa, as follows:

(α) *Initial situation.* Perrault tells of a king and a queen, who desperately wanted a baby, and finally gives birth to a child. The Princess, who has no name, has as godmothers all the kingdom's fairies, who are thought to be seven. They all participate in the girl's baptism and later go to the palace for a magnificent feast. As everybody eats and drinks, an old Fairy, who had not been invited, suddenly arrives.

(E³) *Reconnaissance by others to obtain information about the villain.* The uninvited guest is an old Fairy, who was forgotten because it had been over fifty years since she had been seen out of a tower. Therefore, everybody thought her dead or enchanted.

(λ) *Preliminary misfortune.* After six of the fairies have given their gifts to the Princess, the old Fairy (villain) predicts that she will have her hand pierced by a spindle and die of the wound. A young fairy had been waiting to give her gift after the wicked fairy, so she could eventually repair as much evil as possible. In her turn, she affirms that, although she has no powers to completely undo what the ancient has done, she can make it so that instead of dying, the Princess will fall into a profound sleep which would last a hundred years. At the expiration of this time, a King's son would come to awaken her.

(A) Villainy—the casting of a spell. Fifteen or sixteen years later (Perrault does not locate the date precisely). Despite the King's decree forbidding any kind of spindles in his castles and houses, the Princess finds a good old woman on the top of a tower spinning with her spindle. Attracted by the novelty, she asks to try it and the old woman, never having heard anything about the king's proclamation, lets the girl do it. The Princess pricks her finger.

(-) Negative result. She then falls into a deep sleep. The good fairy arrives, and puts everything and everyone in the kingdom—except the king and the queen who leave—to sleep to be awakened one hundred years hence after the Princess.

(↑) Departure from home. At the expiration of the one hundred years, a Prince is out hunting. Perrault explains that he is the son of the reigning king, coming from a different family than that of the princess. Seeing a tower in the middle of the woods, he asks his entourage about it, and the people answer with different stories that they have heard. Some say it is inhabited by spirits; others say, by sorcerers, still others, by an Ogre. Finally, someone tells him the true version. This sets the prince on fire: he thinks that he must to be the Princess's hero.

(G²) Transference to a designated place. The prince rides to the castle and arrives at the Princess's chamber moved by curiosity and attraction for her supposed beauty.

(K⁴) Liquidation of misfortune as a direct result from action. The prince simply approaches the Princess and trembles with

admiration at the girl's beauty, falling on his knees before her. In the seventeenth century tale, the simple proximity of the prince to the princess awakens her, while in Petipa's ballet, as well as the Grimms,' Disney's and most of subsequent Western versions of the story, the prince, marvelled by her beauty, gives her a kiss, which is what awakens her.

(*K⁹*) *Resuscitation*. The Princess stands up and the whole palace awakens, too. Perrault states: "They did not speak much: little eloquence, a great deal of love. He was more at loss than she was and we need not wonder at it; she had time to think on what to say to him; for it is very probable, (though history mentions nothing of it) that the good fairy, during so long a sleep, had given her very agreeable dreams. In short, they talked four hours together, and yet they did not say half the things they had to say." They then sup in a luxurious way, served by the Princess's officers.

(*W*) *Wedding*. After supper, the couple does not lose time and is immediately married by Lord Almoner in the chapel of the castle. After the wedding, Perrault's version continues with a new move, which creates a new complete cycle, from an act of villainy, to its corresponding *denouement* with the liquidation of misfortune. In Perrault's story, after the wedding, the prince leaves his beloved the next morning to go back to the city and his parent's palace.

(*α*) *Initial situation: presentation of the king and queen*. The prince's father is a good person but his mother is not. By fear of her, the prince does not tell them what happened to him. He invents a story, telling them that he had been lost in the forest and that he had finally spent the night in a good peasant's house.

Temporal determination: two years pass. The prince constantly "goes hunting," and the queen suspects that he has in fact a "little amour". By that time, the prince has already two children with the Princess. They name the first one, a girl, Aurore (Morning), the little boy, Jour (Day), a most powerful name "because he was a great deal more handsome and beautiful than his sister." This phrase typically exemplifies Perrault's sexist favoring of men, who are often more interesting, intelligent and beautiful than the author's female counterparts.

(δ^2) Information about the villain. Although the prince loves his mother, he does not dare to tell her the truth since he knows that she is an ogress. "The king himself would never have married her, had it not been for her vast riches," tells Perrault explaining that, as an Ogress, she attacks little children.

($\uparrow$) Departure from home on a quest. After the king dies, about two years later, the prince decides to present his queen to the palace. Some time later, as so many fairy tale heroes do, he leaves for a war.

(γ) Interdiction. The prince-turned-king, leaves the reign with the Queen Mother, but he prohibits her from touching his family.

(λ) Preliminary misfortune. Nevertheless, as soon as he leaves, the ogress sends her daughter-in-law with the children to a small house in the woods, planning to easily execute her terrible desires.

(A) Villainy. She tells the clerk of the kitchen that she wants Aurore for dinner with Sauce Robert (a typical French sauce made with onions, butter, vinegar, mustard and wine).

(F^6) The Helper (the clerk). The poor man goes to the small house carrying a knife to get the four-year old girl, but he does not have the courage and ends up by concealing the child, killing a little lamb and serving it to the Queen with the best Sauce Robert he could ever make.

(I) Victory over the villain. The Queen greatly appreciated the meal. Here, the helper (clerk) has two more victories over the villain. Eight days later, the same happens with Jour, which the clerk replaced by a young kid, very tender, the Queen

found delicious. Some time later, the wicked Queen also decides to eat the young Queen with the same sauce. The poor cook tries to do it, but without courage, he dressed a hind, and gives it to the Queen, who devours it with the same appetite she had shown previously.

(H) New struggle with the villain. The Queen was pleased with her cruelties and ready to tell her son that his family had been eaten by the crazy wolves. One day, passing by the place where they were hiding, she hears little Jour crying and consequently finds out what had happened. In a frenzy, she fills a tub with snakes, toods, vipers and all kinds of serpents and prepares it to be thrown on to them.

(K⁴) Liquidation of misfortune by direct result of previous action. Before the evil is done, the king suddenly arrives.

(U) Punishment of the villain. The Queen, in panic, throws herself into the tub and is devoured instantly.

The ballet *(α)* presents the royal family and also introduces the grandiosity of their reigns through an astonishing display of a *corps-de-ballet* composed of dancers as fairies. As the curtain rises, a king and a queen enter the stage, followed by a crowd. They carry a baby and six fairies, dressed in different colors, gather around them and perform solos. The last one to dance is the Lilac Fairy, the one dressed in a purple tutu, who does very serene almost staccato arabesques. As she comes close to the cradle, everyone freezes, noticing a small black carriage, where an old woman in a black dress is being led by two men also in black. The strange old woman—"she" is actually a male dancer dressed as female-gets out of it and begins to dance and mime.

(E³) The strange figure is Carabosse, the angry fairy, who is recognized by the way she mimes angry and menacing faces, pointing her finger to the king and queen.

(A) is shown allegorically, in a vision of a young girl dressed as a princess. She arises from a kind of stage basement and stands still like a doll, while Carabosse points at her, miming

the pricking of the finger, and laughing sadistically. Lilac Fairy, then, slowly comes in Carabosse's direction, turning and stopping in arabesque poses that point at her with stretched arms. Her movements are calm but strong and firm. These indicate her taming Carabosse's spell, replacing the princess's death with a sleeping spell.

Act I of the ballet, called "The Spell" embodies the act of villainy. Here, Vsevolovzskhy and Petipa chose to locate the time of the enchantment when the princess is older than the fifteen or sixteen vaguely suggested by Perrault. In the ballet, the event occurs suggestively as the princess celebrates her twentieth birthday, a time when she is to choose a man to marry. Metaphorically, the spell takes place during her rite of passage, from adolescence to womanhood. It becomes a lesson for the princess: a lesson about grace, caution, and the dangers of curiosity.

Princess Aurora, dressed in a pink tutu, dances in front of a line of four men, among whom she should chose a husband. The men bow to her while she keeps taking steps solely towards her parents—in doing so, she seems to be affirming that she does not fancy the men. Her constant arabesques built away from them indicate her superior style and proud personality. When the men rearrange themselves in a line in front of her, Aurora crosses through it, giving her hand quickly to each men while she arabesques, staying in perfectly still poses and never looking at them. Each time the men's hands touch hers, she leaves them and sustains her own arabesques herself—these unsustainable arabesques are not only virtuosic physically but also morally, as she proves to be good and well-behaved (Jowitt, *Time and the Dancing Image*).

While Aurora is later engaged in a solo, an old woman enters the stage carrying a bouquet of flowers. She gives the flowers to Aurora, who starts dancing and turning happily while carrying it. The princess suddenly notices the presence of a long spindle inside the bouquet. She looks at with an expression of curiosity, throws the bouquet away and plays with it, fascinated, posing in various arabesques until she finally pricks her finger. The old woman then bounces her arms back and forth and shakes her fingers, miming the spell she had thrown over the princess.

(-) Aurora feels sorry for her distraction and curiosity as she performs a weeping solo. She realizes and regrets what she had done, using staccato arabesques and gestures miming pain, while the old woman walks after her. Her clothes slip off and we finally recognize her as Carabosse. In this version, it is not a good old woman who happened to be spinning as in Perrault's version. All the evil is created by the wicked fairy.

(↑) Act II marks the departure of the prince to rescue the sleeping princess in the woods. The set design depicts a castle overgrown with ivy, trees, and lilacs becoming an impenetrable forest, and indicating that a century has passed. This serves as a background to a group of people dressed in hunting clothes, the men in leggings, the women in long skirts and hats. They dance a minuet with the prince, who stays in the center of the stage. His movements are particularly virtuosic, composed of jumps and cabriolets, entrechats and turns in the air—demonstrating his brave and athletic character.

The hunting minuets are Petipa's reference to the sixteenth and seventeenth-century *grand ballets* in France. There, despite the growing number of professional dancers who already participated in spectacles, the final *grand ballet* was reserved for the aristocracy alone. This section of the social dance, which had no theme and was purely geometric, was a way to maintain the importance of the nobility in the dance world (Clarke and Crisp 130).

Afterwards, a change in the music occurs, from a happy minuet-like to a slow and lyric melody. This marks the arrival of Fairy Lilac. The prince bows and walks after her while pointing to the background, miming the castle where Aurora is. Dancing a *pas-de-deux* they get acquainted, while other fairies in violet appear in increasing numbers to form a resonating *corps-de-ballet*. In the background, Aurora appears dressed in white and performing slow movements until she comes closer to the prince and dances a *pas-de-deux* with him. From her clothes, the serenity of her dance and the way Lilac points to her, we understand that this is only a vision of the princess, something used by Lilac to convince the prince to follow her on a journey to the castle.

(G^2) The transference to the castle takes place on a boat led by Lilac. As the vision of Aurora disappears a boat crosses the background, with Lilac sitting on it. She makes a sign for the prince to join her. Together, they point towards the castle and the boat moves across the stage, until it disappears.

Petipa and Vsevolozhsky have attributed more power to Lilac than to the prince. While in Perrault's tale, the prince is the one who decides to meet the challenge, here, he needs Lilac to conduct him and even to seduce him with a vision of the beautiful Aurora. When they arrive, Carabosse is guarding the castle against any possible rescuer.

Six fairies appear on the stage in front of Carabosse. Dancing in a threatening way, they force Carabosse to leave. Lilac enters, the lights of upstage are turned on, and we see the princess sleeping over a bed, covered by a web and surrounded by other sleeping people. Behind Aurora's bed, the Prince climbs down the stairs, coming in her direction with vigorous jumps. As he comes closer, the web is raised and finally disappears.

(K^4) Ironically, although the ballet was based on an aristocratic tale written in seventeenth century France, its use of the kiss was not taken from Perrault, who probably would have thought of it as too vulgar. As folklorists Iona and Peter Opie have pointed out, at the time the ballet was created at the end of the nineteenth century, the tale of *Sleeping Beauty* already had a tradition in Western Europe as a pantomime. During that time, the kiss became an important element in the story (105). The kiss was also used in the Brothers Grimm's less aristocratic version, *Little Briar Rose,* and, since Walt Disney, it has appeared in all subsequent Western versions of the tale.

(K^9) Aurora's resuscitation in the ballet is presented mimetically, as she yawns and brings her hand to cover her mouth. She slowly wakes up all the others asleep around her. The prince then kisses her hand; they walk away and the curtain falls.

(W) Act III, the final act of the ballet, marks Aurora's wedding to Prince Desire. Here the young couple with the king and the queen, the fairies and a procession of other Perrault's fairy tale characters perform a *divertissement*. The scenery shows the interior of a palace, with crystal chandeliers and walls decorated with Doric columns.

Little by little, the stage is inhabited by recognizable characters. We first see an old man with a long blue beard followed by a line of women. As he hangs his sword and mimes cutting the women's throats, it becomes clear that he is Bluebeard. Then comes a rabbit, later a man in blue with his stretched arms, imitating the gestures of a bird (Blue Bird), a cat in red boots carrying two small dead rats (Puss-in-Boots). They are followed by a girl in a red peasant dress, carrying a basket with flowers, who dances a *pas-de-deux* with a wolf (Little Red Riding Hood). Then come a couple of big bears followed by a line of small boys.

Afterwards, the music changes and there is a solo for Lilac: she seems to be the real hero of the story in this ballet version. Three other fairies dance together. They wear white tutus but have colored plumes on their heads — golden, blue and white, respectively. We know through the libretto that they are the fairies of gold, sapphire and diamond. Their dance is an allegro: extremely fast and happy, composed of jumps, kicks and turns.

Here the godmother fairies of the beginning are replaced by the fairies of gold, sapphire, and diamond. Prior to the happy ending, there is a direct homage to money, luxury and splendor, elements that symbolically represent aristocratic power. In the background, during the apotheosis, Lilac is performing arabesques while a waterfall springs behind her. When the ballet is over, Lilac is the last to receive the applauses. She is the real heroine, embodying the unique Russian imprint on this glorifying story.

As Wiley puts it, the glorification of King Florestan's reign evokes the style of mid-seventeenth to mid-eighteenth century, with melodies in the spirit of Lully and Rameau. The decor is also late seventeenth-century France. Nevertheless, although the ballet pays homage to Louis XIV's court, it has trademarks that are unmistakably late nineteenth-century Russia.

As much as Perrault's *La Belle au bois dormant,* Vsevolozh-sky/Petipa's *Sleeping Beauty* reflects its time and place, created with a specific point of view. The time is late nineteenth century, the place is Imperialist Russia, and the point of view is that of an aristocracy that is threatened by changes that are beginning to be delineated in the country. This aristocracy is trying to sustain its power and luxurious life style although it feels its anachronism in the face of a devastating economical and political crisis.

In order to understand the relation of the work to its context, we need to examine how the ballet differs in narrative form from Perrault's literary tale. One of the changes comes from Petipa/Vsevolozhsky's decision to give names to the nameless characters of Perrault's tales. The name of the princess has a significance here, not only because Aurore suggests a cycle of life, thereby reinforcing the allegorical tone of the dance, but also because of its precedence vis-a-vis Perrault. In the French writer's version, Aurore is the name of the Princess's daughter. In applying this name, changed to Aurora, to the protagonist of the Russian version, Vsevolozhsky may have wished to connote a direct descent from the lineage of seventeenth-century France of Louis XIV, with the late nineteenth-Russian court of Alexander III, at least in terms of values and protocol.

Another important, yet more subtle change in the translation from literature to ballet is the way the latter significantly enlarged the role played by the fairies and consequently magnified the dichotomy between good and evil. The inclusion of the fairies as characters of the story is associated with Charles Perrault's context, where *féeries* became fashionable in the seventeenth-century French court.

Earlier versions of the tale, as will be shown, did not even contain fairies. The fate of sleeping beauty had been simply a question of tragic destiny, something previewed by generic wise men in the beginning of the story, without connotations of evil beings or vengeful spells. The Grimms' version, intended to appeal less to the aristocracy, also omits fairies. *Little Briar Rose* presents wise women who only appear in the beginning of the story, to make both the good and bad wishes associated with the princess's birth.

In contrast, the ballet *Sleeping Beauty* elaborates on the roles played by both the good and the evil fairies. It uses the wicked fairy not only to throw the initial spell, as in Perrault's book, but also to place Carabosse as the disguised old woman who brings the spindle hidden inside a bouquet of flowers so that the princess can accidentally prick her finger. Later, Carabosse is also the one who guards the castle, with her evil crew, against anybody who may come and eventually try to break the spell. She is the omnipresent evil.

The same growth of roles applies to the good fairies. In the ballet, what motivates the prince to get to the castle where the princess lies asleep is not simply curiosity and excitement, as it is in Perrault's book. In Petipa's version, he is guided by Fairy Lilac, who also shows him the vision of the princess, to ensure that he is indeed going towards her. Finally, Lilac is the one who closes the whole story, arabesquing victoriously in a solo before the curtain falls at the end of the performance.

The ballet uses Perrault's fairies and enlarges their parts for different reasons. First, *ballet-féeries* were fashionable at that time, with the image of the post-romantic ballerina transformed into an aerial and otherworldly being, able to turn and almost to fly. Second and most importantly, the Manichean dichotomy that the fairies embody reinforces the ballet's allegorical aspect. The wicked fairy is evil. She is old, ill-dressed and rude. Metaphorically, she symbolizes a lapse in the royal protocol, in which the king forgets to invite one of the fairies. In contrast, the good fairy is serene and beautiful, and she stands behind Aurora to guarantee that she will remain well-mannered and avoid coquetteries during her twentieth birthday. She also commands the fairies of money—gold and sapphire.

Another obvious and crucial change in the course of the narrative from literature to ballet, is the exclusion of the last part of Perrault's tale. The ballet ends in a farcical display, with the participation of all Perrault's characters, who become guests at the princess's wedding. The wedding celebration is stretched to a point where it is turned into a luxurious *divertissement*.

This procedure can be understood in many ways. It was mainly an excuse for pure visual display, as well as a way to use a large number of dancers who worked for the czar as dancers of the Maryinsky ballet company. It was also a way to pay homage to Perrault's work and, consequently, to Louis XIV's epoch. Thus, it marked the pomp, the luxury, the absolute power of the monarch, and on a entertainment level, *la mode des contes de fée*.

In the ballet *Sleeping Beauty* there is no need for Ogress mothers and cannibalist attempts. The message is already transmitted with the wedding, with no need for Perrault's epilogue. The abandonment of this second part was a decision also endorsed by the subsequent version by the Brothers Grimm, the filmic version by Walt Disney and the all the popularized written versions of the tale in the Western world. In fact, the way Charles Perrault structured his tale, separating the story in two parts that seem incongruent, embodies a narrative solution that hides unacceptable behaviors vis-a-vis his moral values. He had created, for example, an evil mother with cannibalist habits, a wicked behavior more expected from a stepmother.

Nevertheless, if we examine the written source for Perrault's tale, his narrative options seem more clear. The French writer was acquainted with an earlier version by Neapolitan writer Giambattista Basile, called "Sun, Moon and Talia," which was part of his sixteenth-century collection, the *Pentamerone*. Between this time and the late seventeenth century in France, great changes in moral rules and sexual behavior occurred, and Perrault was sensitive to these changes.

In the sixteenth-century Neapolitan tale, Talia is newly-born and her king father is advised by wise men that she would die of a pricked finger. Although her father avoids everything similar in the kingdom, she finds a spinning wheel and pricks her finger. She dies and is abandoned in the castle by her father. A king out hunting, arrives at the castle and, surprised by the beauty of her insensible body, rapes her, leaves her and forgets about the whole incident. Nine months later, she gives birth to twins, a boy and a girl. Although Talia is insensible, the children feed themselves at her breast. One day, the boy mistakenly sucks her finger, drawing out the splinter that was stuck in it, giving her life again. Later, the same king, passing by the castle by chance, finds out what had happened and forms a "great league" with his illegitimate family—he was already married before the incident. The queen guesses what has happened and plots to kill her husband's illegitimate children. By a ruse she obtains possession of the children and consigns them to the cook, ordering him to make her husband a meal with them. The cook has a good heart and substitutes for the children with other meat. Later, the queen also tries to kill Talia, and she is about to do it when the king arrives and saves his true beloved.

Proceeding from an oral tradition, the tale of *Sleeping Beauty* later evolved within the literary tradition. Basile's tale was based on a fifteenth- century manuscript called *Perceforest*, created by an anonymous writer. Chapter forty-six of this book tells the story of Princess Zellandine, who pricks her finger while spinning and then falls asleep. Her lover Troylus comes to the tower where she sleeps, gives way to his sexual desire and nine months later, Zellandine gives birth to a baby. When the child mistakes her finger for her nipple, he sucks the spindle out of it and she awakens.

In the version written by Charles Perrault, the act of violation of a woman presented in both the *Perceforest* and the *Pentamerone*, are mythicized and ideologically transformed, to become, instead, an act of salvation. As Jack Zipes explained in *The Brothers Grimm*, prior to the seventeenth century, it was commonly accepted for a princes to take adbvantadge of a sleeping, defenseless woman. By Perrault's time this behavior was not openly accepted, so the author rewrote the tale in a baroque fashion (152).

At the same time, Perrault left the cannibalist aspects of the story, with the second part involving the ogress mother. In nineteenth century, ogresses were considered too gross and vulgar and, therefore, the ballet dropped this part of the fairy tale. Nevertheless, it kept Perrault's message intact and perfectly suitable to the country's czarist context. There is indeed a clear lineage of versions, from Perrault to the Grimms, to Vsevolozhsky/Petipa, to Walt Disney and most of the anonymous nursery collections currently produced. These rewritten fairy tales are all mythicized products, inverting the values of previous manuscripts as to suit their specific moral codes. All the "classical" versions of *Sleeping Beauty* that we know have inverted the act of violation, and worked it out into salvation so it became a lesson of moral and sexual behavior, pacience and docility.

The implications of the glorification of King Florestan in the ballet are complex and even ambiguous, if we consider that the reproduction of the Louis XIV style is not so faithful. As Wiley suggests, while in France Lully and his collaborators forbade the inclusion of anything unflattering to Louis XIV, the ballet's King Florestan has an incompetent Master of Ceremonies, who makes a mistake in protocol forgetting to invite one of the fairies. Florestan's lack of control in avoiding violations of etiquette in the reign could be related to the political situation under Alexander III. During that time, Russia was for many years under martial law to control a devastating economic crisis and consequent political upheavals (Raeff 190).

At the end of the ballet, Vsevolozhsky and Petipa allegorically replaced personal values for material ones. This is exemplified in the substitution of the six good fairies at the beginning of the dance for fairies representing wealth—the fairies of gold and sapphire are the ones who eventually dance a *pas-de-quatre* with Aurora and the prince. Final credit is given to money.

The implied criticism of the czarist reign could be confirmed in the emperor's cool reaction to the work. In the assembling of the ballet, Petipa knew how to use allegorical and ironic elements, confirming his lineage with Perrault, himself a master of irony. The latter, for example, combined the evil habits of the ogress with the French Sauce Robert and used his fairy tales to establish models of behavior, praising the woman who could wait one hundred years for her beloved husband.

4

The Fairy Tale Revisited:
From Sleeping Beauty to the
Postmodern Fairy Tale

Fairies on Pointe

Although earlier productions of fairy tale ballets were registered in dance history books and dictionaries—for example, *Cinderella* was choreographed by Charles Didelot for the Paris Opera Ballet in 1823 (Terry)—the genre blossomed with Petipa's monumental pieces based on literary fairy tales in the late nineteenth century. These included *Sleeping Beauty* (1890), *The Nutcracker*, choreographed with his assistant Lev Ivanon (1892), *Cinderella* (1893), created with Ivanov and Italian dancer/choreographer Enrico Cechetti, *Bluebeard* (1896) and *The Magic Mirror* (1903).

The romantic era of the beginning of nineteenth century Europe, with its infatuation with the supernatural and the ethereal ideal of the ballerina certainly set the ground for the fairy tale ballet format. But it was with Petipa that fairy tales turned into a prototype for ballet librettos. Besides knowing how to use this enduring attraction to the supernatural, Petipa managed to parallel the fairy tale magical shifts in the narrative plot with the actual virtuoso shifts of postures demanded by the ballet steps.

The choreographer also depicted male and female dancers in a contrasting manner that reinforced gender notions in vogue at that time. Indeed, Petipa's way of portraying men and women relationships onstage has been frozen in time and perpetuated in the balletic world from then on. Within the development of ballet as a theatrical form, the ballerina had become the center of attention. She was increasingly given jumps, turns and arabesques, while her male counterpart was limited onstage to being her porteur.

But this preponderant female exposure was far from being a sign of power. First, all the powerful positions within the ballet world, from choreographer to producer, were kept exclusively for men. Second, the content of the librettos endorsed male superiority. During the early nineteenth- century, ballet romantic era, although leading roles were given to female characters, it was the men who acted in the stories. In *La Sylphide* and *Giselle*, the key works of that era, it was the men, James and Albrecht, respectively, who carried on the problems in the plots, made the choices and acted, while the female characters were passive (Aschengreen 30).

Paraphrasing what was to become George Balanchine's most popular phrase, Petipa also saw ballet as a woman (Daly, "Classical Ballet". In Petipa's dances, the *corps-de-ballet* is composed of large crowds of female dancers, all moving in unison, echoing gestures in such a perfect way, they seem to impersonate the notion of dance as a feminized art per se.

In a world of adagios and arabesques, where the ballerinas played more roles than their male counterparts, it might be assumed that Petipa attributed dominance to women. The Petipa ballerina is indeed the center of attention; nevertheless, she is a virtuosic object of beauty manipulated by her more active yet less exposed male counterpart (Daly, "Classical Ballet").

Petipa's ballerinas have an status that is equivalent to that of fairy tale heroines in the literary stories, particularly since Charles Perrault. In the fairy tale collections, stories are told in a way to guarantee that women are beautiful, vulnerable, passive and obedient. In her body of work, feminist Kay Stone stresses that, in the Grimms and Disney stories, these characteristics are preconditions for a woman to be a heroine.

Sleeping Beauty has to wait patiently one hundred years to be awakened by her prince. The Petipa ballerina has to display cunningly her dancing skills until a *porteur* comes to manipulate and support her. It is only then that these women become heroines or dancing stars.

Not only did the gender format endorsed by Petipa become universally accepted and adopted in ballet over the years. The popular signification of ballet is equated with the realization of music in a balanced and symmetrical arrangement of space. These are in themselves characteristics of Petipa's classical ballet language. Over time, ballet has become an experience of high culture, as well as a feminized art that focuses on grace, purity and civility.

Although they evolved in response to historical circumstances and the particular genius of creators like Petipa, these notions of ballet became "mythicized." They overturned culture into nature, substituting characteristics that were products of cultural, historical and ideological contexts into the idea of the "natural" way, the way ballet is meant to be (Barthes).

The notions of ballet as a graceful, pure and feminized art became "classical," universal and anonymously attributed in the same way that tales such as *Cinderella* or *Sleeping Beauty* have been transcribed in fairy tale collections over and over again without any attribution of authorship or social context. It is "naturally" accepted that *Sleeping Beauty* is a story about a princess who, after one hundred years of sleep, is awakened by a prince. It does not matter that this is only a version of a tale, recreated by a particular author in the context of seventeenth-century France. Nor does it matter that the earlier versions of this tale proved that this was a story of rape.

The same "mythicization" echoed in the ballet world. After Petipa, the fairy tale was consecrated as a thematic source and continued to reappear in the repertory of the most important ballet companies worldwide. Its success responds to an infallible formula which combines well-known stories to which audiences can relate. They are stories filled with magic adventures, which allow the pieces to become virtuosic showcases.

Examples of fairy tales turned into ballet productions abound. The first of George Balanchine's ballets to be shown in Paris in 1925 was *The Song of the Nightingale,* based on Hans Christian Andersen's tale. *The Fairy's Kiss* was choreographed by Balanchine in 1937 for the American Ballet and by Frederic Ashton for the Sadler's Wells (now the Royal Ballet), while *Beauty and the Beast* was choreographed by John Crancko, also for the Sadler's Wells in 1949. *Bluebeard*, after Petipa, was conceived by Michel Fokine in 1941 and produced by the Ballet Theater.

Other specific fairy tales were used in even a larger number of productions. After Didelot and the 1893 Saint Petersburg production by Cecchetti, Ivanov and Petipa, with music by Boris Shell and libretto by Lidia Pashkova, *Cinderella* was produced in 1938, choreographed by Michel Fokine for the Original Ballet Russe, with music by Frederic d'Elenger and scenery by Natalia Gontcharova. There was also a 1945 production by Zakharov for the Bolshoi Ballet in Moscow, this one being the first to use Prokofiev's score; and also American productions, beginning with the one created for the National Ballet of Washington by Ben Stevenson in 1970.

Peter and the Wolf, considered a contemporary fairy tale, as it was created by Sergei Prokofiev himself in 1936 for orchestra, had a first ballet version conceived by Adolph Bolm for the Ballet Theater in 1940. Many other productions followed such as Ivo Cramer's for the Norwegian National Ballet, Niels B. Larsen for the Royal Danish Ballet, a 1969 version choreographed by Jacques D'Amboise for the New York City Ballet and a 1991 adapted version by Michael Smuin for the American Ballet Theater.

Sleeping Beauty, after Petipa, was choreographed by Bronislava Nijinska, as well as by Sergeyev for the Sadler's Wells in 1946, and it has an additional version choreographed by Frederick Ashton and Ninette de Valois. Finally, *The Nutcracker*, after Ivanov under Petipa's auspices, was choreographed by Sergeyev for the Sadler's Wells in 1934, first presented in American through a production of the Ballet Russes de Monte Carlo in 1940, and restaged by Balanchine for the New York City Ballet in 1954.

From the Modernist Myth to the PostModern Fairy Tale

While the fairy tale became almost a paradigm for ballet, it was eventually rejected by the modern dance world. The modernist project in dance corresponded less to the experiments with abstraction developed in the visual arts, for example, and more to a search for essential emotions, social engagement and expressive movements.

Reacting against the weightless, ethereal quality of ballet, modern dance emphasized deep emotions, bare feet and a strong relationship with the ground and the world. Similarly, reacting against what was to be considered ballet's light, almost infantile themes—namely, fairy tales—modern dance emphasized adult drama.

In the thirties and forties, American choreographers such as Martha Graham and Doris Humphrey denied ballet's tendency to become a superficial entertainment and a virtuosic showcase. In their particular ways, these choreographers brought expression back to the center of dance. As Selma Jeanne Cohen said, Graham looked inwards, to the individual's relation to his own feelings and experiences, while her former colleague in Denishaw, Doris Humphrey, looked out at the individual's relation to the world around him (*Dance as a Theater Art* 121).

In opposition to the fairy tale motif of classical ballet, Graham choreographed a cycle of dances based on Greek mythology which, in a way, revisited a tradition in dance history. But while mythology was a prototypical theme for choreographies in Renaissance Europe because of its association with classical Greek and high culture, suitable to the aristocracy, Graham used it in ways that were totally different. She saw myths as archetypes of universal emotions such as passion, guilt and redemption, as well as symbolic marks of life's cycle. Graham's mythological phase began with *Herodiade* (1946) and was climaxed with *Clytemnestra* (1958), her most ambitious undertaking of the phase. As Marcia Siegel has pointed out, Graham's work at that time was epic, declamatory, and Graham dancers made statements (Siegel, *Shapes of Change* 191).

In contrast, during the sixties and seventies, the urge for expression and drama launched by the modern dancers was questioned and eventually abandoned by a new generation of choreographers known as the Judsonites or the postmodern dance choreographers. During its initial developments, postmodernism in dance did not refer to the notions of historical references, *pastiche*, irony, and nostalgia that are attributes associated to the post-modern condition in cultural history, philosophy and art. In fact, the term "postmodern dance" has been coined by some dance critics, particularly Sally Banes and Noel Carroll, in reference to a generation's reaction to modern dance as it was propagated by choreographers such as Martha Graham, Doris Humphrey and José Limon.

Placing it into context, the discoveries and changes brought by the postmodern generation in dance dealt with issues mostly associated with modernism in the other fields of art and culture. These issues included the acknowledgement of the medium's mechanics and materials, the formal and functional aspects of dance, as well as a preoccupation with abstraction and austerity.

In her book *Terpsichore in Sneakers*, Sally Banes situates the denial of narrative and drama within a period in postmodern dance that she calls analytic, occurring particularly in the early seventies. This phase is marked by the work of choreographers such as Yvonne Rainer, Trisha Brown, David Gordon, Douglas Dunn and others. As Banes affirms, the analytic postmodern dance displayed modernist preoccupations with abstraction and aligned itself with modernist visual art and minimalist sculpture (xv).

Reacting against the expressionism of modern dance, which connected dance with narrative, music, visual and literary ideas, these postmodern choreographers began to propose that the formalist quality of dance could be reason enough for choreography (Banes 15). Another analytical postmodern dance motto was the use of pedestrian movements and clothing, a reaction against the elitist condition imposed by specifically trained bodies. For the postmodern choreographers at that time, real movement was movement undistorted for the sake of theatrical effectiveness of emotional expressiveness. The analytic postmodern dance slogan, "Less is More," is significantly illustrated in a statement written by Yvonne Rainer in 1965, which she called "manifesto of renunciation" (1965):

NO to spectacle no to virtuosity no to transformation and magic and make believe no to the glamour and transcendency of the star image no to the heroic no to the anti-heroic no to trash imagery no to involvement of performer or spectator no to style no to camp no to seduction of spectator by the wiles of the performer no to eccentricity no to moving or being moved (Rainer 1965).

Rejecting the idea that dance should be expressive, the early generation of postmodern choreographers created dances which did not provide the spectators with opportunities for narrative identification. This result was achieved by the use of anti-illusionist procedures. Illusionism in art is the capacity to connect the spectator on a diegesic level of relationship with the work. Put another way, it corresponds to the work's magical, systematic and revelatory capacity of presenting meaning (Trachtenberg 7).

In her "Trio A—The Mind is a Muscle" (1966), for example, Rainer dealt with made-up movements, performed in a pedestrian way. She presented the dance within a neutral posture and facial expression, which increased the distance between performers and audiences. In early postmodern dance, illusionistic effects were also discouraged by the choice of work clothing or sweat suits instead of leotards and traditional dance costumes; by minimal or repetitive movements; and by an emphasis on the effort these movements required, which revealed the refusal to differentiate the dancer's body from that of the ordinary person (Trachtenbeg 8).

Of course, parallel to these experiments there were still choreographers working with narrative and emotions. Not every choreographer belonging to the Judson Memorial Church group followed the same approach to dance and phases in the development of their work showed different concerns and ways of dealing with the medium. Nevertheless, postmodern dance is commonly associated with the denial of narrative and drama.

Currently however, narrative made a come back and became the center of preoccupations of the new dance generation. Following a chronological survey of tendencies, the new generation of postmodern dance is again attracted to telling stories. Particularly since the eighties, postmodern choreographers have been again infatuated with content, meaning and historical references, a procedure that connects the dance world with the other fields of postmodern art, philosophy and culture.

This infatuation with narrative and meaning is discussed in many articles by dance critics. For example, Deborah Jowitt wrote an article titled, "The Return of Drama—A Postmodern Strategy?" (1984) and Noel Carroll published "The Return of the Repressed—The Re-Emergence of Expression in Contemporary American Dance" (1984). To differentiate this generation from analytic post-modern dance of the seventies, Sally Banes calls this tendency "new dance." New dance choreographers are mainly preoccupied with meaning, although they still engage in formal questions about the nature and function of the dance medium—a concern typical of the choreographers of the sixties and seventies ("New Dance" 52).

Banes explains that narrative was reborn in the eighties in a way that is nevertheless not a simple return to older values or techniques of storytelling. The way the new generation deals with narrative incorporates the development of post-modern dance in its deliberate dismantling of literary devices, fragmentation and ambiguity of interpretation. In contrast to the theatrical illusions fostered by Martha Graham or Doris Humphrey, the new choreographers create pieces that are partially expressive and partially abstract, playing with perception and interpretation (*Terpsichore* xxxi).

At the same time, the new generation's infatuation with stories relates to a generalized postmodern attraction for convention, nostalgia and storytelling witnessed in other fields of art, academia and popular culture. The philosophical trends of post-structuralism and deconstruction imposes the notion of text above everything else.

The return to stories can also be seen as a response to an era of political and economic insecurity. The Judson artists were working during the 1960's and 1970's within the growing authority of the doctrine "less is more." Nevertheless, this sense of artistic community soon began to deteriorate. The 1980's, the Reagan era, saw a regrowth of consumerism, and a fascination with opulence, illustrated in television series like "Dallas" and "Dynasty" (Trachtenberg 12-14).

In opposition to the experiments with abstraction, the consistent use of narrative is becoming an anchor for representation, with the audiences being given recognizable material, which guarantees that they will remain consuming the artistic product. This impulse is paralleled in other artistic fields. For instance, in painting, postmodern artists like David Hockney, Brunio Civitico, Peter Blake, James Valerio, David Salle and Michael Mazur are working with figurativism, which Charles Jencks calls "the new classicism".

For an appetite for meaning, cultural conventions and historical references, fairy tales appear as the exemplary narrative. For a generation of folklorists, literary critics and Western structuralists inspired by Propp's *Morphology of the Folktale* (English translation, 1958), the folktale, and in particular the *Marchen*, or fairy tale, were seen not only as a type, but as a prototype for narratives in general. Linda Dégh explains that the fairy tale is a document of human history that compares to the zone-rings of a very old tree trunk. The evolution of the *Marchen* motifs offers a precious account of our cultural evolution ("Folk Narrative").

The new folklorists and literary critics who search for meaning in the tale beyond either its morphology or its style, correspond in dance to the later generation of choreographers, who insist that dance has content—in particular, historical and social content. As Sally Banes points out, twenty years after the impact of Propp and Levi-Strauss, folklore and critical theory has turned away from form, toward an analysis of content, performance, context and reception (Banes, "Happily Ever After"). Alan Dundes, Jack Zipes, and their colleagues are part of this generation that tries to articulate the significance of fairy tales within its socio-historical, cultural, formal and poetic sides.

In dance, the impulse is analogous. After choreographers like Trisha Brown, David Gordon, Yvonne Rainer and others focused on the dance medium itself, the generation that blossomed in the eighties is obsessed with narrative, historicity, emotional content. Many choreographers are particularly concerned with fairy tales. In this case, their artistic focus is not on the telling of the tale, but in the experiments about how to narrate it. These choreographers profit from the fact that fairy tales are well-known narrative frames and consequently play with them, using these frames to question artistic media, the relation of "high" art to mass culture, gender roles, social and political issues in general. As Sally Banes attests, another reason for the new appeal of fairy tales in dance is the postmodern infatuation with the past and its traditions, which has recreated the new choreographers' interest in working in the balletic arena. To work in this arena means not only to try the technique and appropriate the scale of the opera house, but also experiment with ballet's most cherished themes (Banes, "Happily Ever After").

The contemporary use of fairy tales as a dance subject, as opposed to their use in nineteenth-century ballet, is an aesthetic choice related to the postmodern sensibility. In the "Introduction" to *The Postmodern Moment*, Stanley Trachtenberg defines the postmodern project as a way of experimenting with conventional ways of framing experience. This is done in a way as to remove experience from its recognizable contexts. The result is a skeptical attitude toward illusion and coherence of any sequence of actions (6-7).

Pina Bausch has been an inspiration for a whole new generation of postmodern choreographers in Europe and the United States—both Marin and Kinematic have been influenced by *tanztheater* aesthetics. Young American choreographers, like Jane Comfort, say that the presentation of harsh emotional content by Bausch's pieces worked, in the early eighties, as a permission for them to make use of emotion too, as opposed to keeping dance as an structural, abstract art (Jowitt Seminar 1988).

Unlike fairy tale ballets, Bausch's *Bluebeard* does not follow a narrative line imposed by the music. Using only tape-recorded spurts of Bela Bartok's one act opera, *Bluebeard's Castle*, it develops an onslaught of movement metaphors for the impasse between the sexes.

In France, Maguy Marin has choreographed a new version of *Cinderella* (1985) for the Lyon Opera Ballet. Marin, who belongs to a new generation of French choreographers named *danse nouvelle*, has a background that combines classical ballet, her modern dance training with Maurice Bejart and a great appetite for the theater. Her *Cinderella* seems ambiguous as, on the one hand, it reflects the aesthetic innovations brought by the new generation, particularly in the use of different media onstage, while on the other hand, it revisits French balletic tradition.

In fact, at first glance, Marin's *Cinderella* seems a cheerful, delicate ballet, with dancers as masked dolls retelling Perrault's fairy tale. The piece has indeed more ballet steps than other of Marin's works as it was choreographed for ballet-trained dancers rather than for her own company. In a more thorough look, however, it becomes clear that Marin has not created another *Cinderella* ballet. Her work is loaded with an ironic comment about our notions of prettiness, happiness and childhood.

In the United States, many choreographers have been using fairy tale in jigsaw-puzzled, playful ways, combining a generalized excitement towards storytelling, with the pure formalist interplays developed by their postmodern predecessors of the 1960's and 1970's. Kinematic's *The Handless Maiden* (1987), based on the Grimm's *The Girl Without Hands* is a good example of that approach.

This tale, published in the Grimms' collection, is more complex and less well-known than *Sleeping Beauty*, *Cinderella* or *Bluebeard*. *The Girl Without Hands* tells the story of a miller who makes a deal and is trapped by the devil—he has to cut off the hands of his own daughter who washes her hands so well that the devil can not get a hold on her. After she has her hands cut off, she abandons her father and leaves for a forest. There she marries a king and when he leaves for a war, she has a baby. The devil intercepts her letter to the king at the battleground and replaces it with another, saying she had given birth to a monster. The king, furious, tells his mother to kill the girl/queen. She, nevertheless, runs away to another forest, where she finds a fairy who makes her hands grow back again. When the king returns and realizes his mistake, he goes on a seven-year journey and ends up by finding his wife and child.

Kinematic (Tamar Kotoske, Maria Lakis and Mary Ritcher) chose to deconstruct the complex fairy tale text. The women initially cut off the pages of the fairy tale book in a vertical line and subsequently used half of it. In the performance, they have it spoken by an off-stage narrator's voice which accompanies their movement. The performers' gestures are by no means consistently denotative with the story. The overall result is a fascinating interplay of fragmented text and abstract movement that together, clash and mesh, creating new meanings.

Choosing fairy tales as a source and resource for narrative, Kinematic's choreographers, Maguy Marin and Pina Bausch are creating aesthetic revisions, structuring their works within a continuum in dance history. They return to the tradition of nineteenth-century Russia, where fairy tales were typical narrative forms, ingeniously articulated by the choreographer Marius Petipa and used as cultural artifices to exemplify aesthetic, moral and political notions. While Petipa's ballets allegorically reproduced the ideals of the Russian court, the new dance fairy tales also tell a story outside the literary plot. The fairy tale dances reflect values typically embodied in the late seventies and eighties within their own background and cultural milieu.

5

Cinderella As A Battle of Toys

Marin and the Dance Tradition in France

Maguy Marin is one of the leading choreographers of the eclectic *danse nouvelle* movement in France. In order to discuss this eclecticism and its significance in the work of the new generation of choreographers, it is important to understand that modern dance is a new phenomenon in France. While in America and Germany, modernism started to flourish by the beginning of the century—with the experiments of Loie Fuller, Isadora Duncan, Ted Shawn and Ruth Saint-Denis, on the one continent, and Mary Wigman and Rudolf von Laban, on the other—the movement in France is less than twenty years old.

There are many reasons for this delay, in a country that has been the center of European art and culture since the early Renaissance and that, in the beginning of this century, housed avant-garde ballet companies such as Serge Diaghilev's *Ballet Russes*. Among the two main reasons are the strong ballet tradition and the lack of support and public interest for modern dance in the country. In France, until the mid-1970s, only ballet was recognized as an art form. In *La Danse, Naissance d'Un Mouvement de Pensée*, Marcelle Michel, dance critic of *Le Monde*, endorses this argument, attesting that ballet is an art form in perfect accord with the French spirit (25-31).

Since its early developments in the sixteenth and seventeenth centuries, ballet became an aristocratic cultural artifact. It was eventually adopted by the newly rich bourgeoisie, particularly after the 1789 Revolution. Following the Revolutionary period, Napoleon also adopted dance as his favorite art form and began sponsoring grandiloquent productions, where choreographic motifs linked to heroic antiquity were used to legitimate his political power. At that same time, in cabarets and cafes, the boulevard theater genre was developed. There, new themes and motifs, such as the ones depicting witches and fairies brought the genre close to the romantic ballet movement.

When romanticism became old-fashioned, French audiences discovered the exuberance of the new ballet from Russia, brought to Paris by Diaghilev and his *Ballet Russes*. The explosion of colors of Russian artists Roheric, Bakst and Benois's sets and costumes, the exoticism of Russian primitive themes, like that of *Petrouscka* choreographed by Michel Fokine, and the harshly innovative movement vocabulary created by Nijinsky in works like *L'Apres Midi d'Un Faune* and *Le Sacre du Printemps* gave new dimensions to the French artistic scene.

Nevertheless, with the death of Diaghilev, the French dance scene experimented a revitalization of tradition. Serge Lifar, one of the last choreographers of Diaghilev's *Ballets Russes*, went to work at the Paris Opera, where he choreographed for thirty years, turning from modernism into a classicist style of ballet dancing.

With *la libération* at the end of the Second World War, French institutional arts were highly esteemed. A new ballet company, called *Ballet des Champs Elysées* was created under the direction of choreographer Roland Petit. Petit personalized the French ballet dancing style through the flamboyant talent of his star, Zizi Jeanmarie, who wore shorts and pants with pointe shoes.

In the fifties, a new figure became sovereign on the French dance scene: Maurice Béjart. Still drawing from ballet technique, but using it originally through idiosyncratic interpretations of metaphysical texts, Béjart became in fact the greatest guru of modern dance in Europe. Settled in Brussels, where he ran his *Ballet du XX Siècle*, Béjart began to embody a new way of conceiving dance. His *Symphonie Pour Un Homme Seul*, presented in 1955 at the Thêatre de la Monnaie, raised dance to a ritualistic level and turned it into a very popular art.

Nevertheless, Béjart did not continue to innovate. His intellectually-based, large-group choreographies began to depend increasingly upon virtuosic balletic technique. He ceased to develop the French modern dance project. In the early sixties, the only way the French contacted radically experimental dance was through the presence of American choreographers such as Merce Cunningham, who taught workshops in the Francoise and Domninique Dupy studio in Paris.

Much has changed in the last twenty years. Nowadays, contemporary dance has become a sparkling national product. With no direct affinity to any pre-existing style, *danse nouvelle* is now seen as a movement as distinctively French as postmodern dance is American or *butoh* is Japanese. Although the ground had already been broken with the social re-thinkings brought by the "revolution" of 1968, the actual foundation for *danse nouvelle* was laid in 1974, when American modern dancer Carolyn Carlson was elected star choreographer of the Paris Opera.

The French state witnessed the abundant creativity of national contemporary dance and played a key role in its development. In 1978, it financed the *Centre de Danse Contemporaine*, established in Angers, presided by Nikolais and Viola Farber, and two years later, it inaugurated the *Maison de la Danse* in Lyon. Additionally, since 1982, the French Ministry of Culture subsidizes many companies throughout the country. Today, as the *Rencontres de Bagnolet* (former *Concours de Bagnolet*), the barometer of French contemporary dance, celebrates twenty years, choreographers, critics and the public witness the results of the superb evolution of French new dance. One now speaks of a *dance d'auteur*, as one speaks of a *film d'auteur*, evidencing its popularity as an art form. Written works about dance abound in France. Three specialist magazines — *Danser*, *Pour la Danse* and *Saisons de la Danse* — are on newsstands, while the book market has expanded with the publishing of important collections of critical essays, as well as recent biographies of French choreographers Dominique Bagouet, Jean-Claude Gallota and Regine Chopinot. And, with the establishment of the *Théâtre de la Ville* as a performance space principally dedicated to dance, new dance choreographers have gained a large and faithful public.

And how is *danse nouvelle* characterized? After digesting the abstraction of American dance, perceived mainly through the works of Alvin Nikolais, Merce Cunningham and Trisha Brown, and the expressionistic trends of both German *tanztheater* and Japanese *butoh*, the French dance has embodied a new type of narrative dance, where emotional content is the source of choreography, although *mise-en-scènes* are carefully built by formalist gestures. Critic Allen Robertson explained that, although French artists and dancers admire and respect the American postmodern movement, it is proven to be too austere and self-referential for French tastes. Their love for the avant-garde does not extend to art for art's sake (103-109).

Marguerite Marin was born in Toulouse in 1951. Her parents, Spanish political refugées, were exiled in Southern France during Spain's Civil War. Counterbalancing the stark values that she learned from her communist and atheist education, Marin had a colorful childhood in Toulouse, where singing and dancing were part of everyday life.

Marin's formal dance education started out traditionally: when she was eight, she began studying ballet at the *Conservatoire de Toulouse*. One of the crucial influences on Marin's development at that point was Nina Vyroubova, an ex-dancer for the companies of Roland Petit, the *Ballet du Marquis de Cuevas* and the Paris Opera Ballet. Vyroubova added a poetic approach to the technical aspects of ballet dancing, a characteristic that would soon be reflected in Marin's taste for rich theatrical imagery. Following a typical ballerina's path, Marin was engaged as a dancer at a classical company, the Strasbourg Opera Ballet, where she stayed for one year.

At that time, already unsatisfied with the limitations of the classical vocabulary, Marin began searching for other ways of presenting expressive material onstage. She wanted to learn skills that went beyond dancing. That is what she found at Maurice Béjart's *Mudra* school in Brussels. The Sanskrit word *Mudra* means gesture, and Béjart defined it as "thought made flesh, the abstract expression of the soul that moves the little finger and reveals the power of signs, the tangible that becomes the living witness of the inexpressible" (Béjart 243).

There, Marin studied alternative dance techniques, as well as singing, acting and Eastern philosophy and arts.

Within *Mudra*, she participated in the creation of an independent group, named *Chandra*. There, under the leadership of Micha van Hoecke, Marin experimented with new possibilities of choreographing, combining diverse expressive languages. After graduating from the school, the choreographer joined Béjart's *Ballet du XX Siècle* with which she danced for five years. From the Marseille-born choreographer and guru of the European dance, Marin learned lessons of professionalism, discipline and a taste for the spectacular, as well as a concern with intellectual sources and social meanings attached to choreography.

Nevertheless, Marin disagreed with Bejart's technique-oriented, virtuosic and glamorous style. It was American dancer/choreographer Carolyn Carlson, with whom she had worked during the summer of 1974 in Paris, who introduced Marin to the modernist concern with the hidden aspects of dance, which refers to the non-visible emotional intentions that give strength to each gesture (Marin, personal interview, 1990).

Added to her background and direct influences, Marin's work has been marked by artistic personalities whom she admires. Among these are Pina Bausch, for her refusal to limit or label her work within one specific category; director Peter Brook, for his versatility and for his poetic theatrical images; and filmmaker Luis Bunuel, for his fragmented, rich and powerful filmic narratives (Marin, personal interview, 1990).

Apart from her individual style, Marin shares artistic concerns with the new generation of French choreographers who have created *danse nouvelle*. These concerns could be broadly summarized as a belief that individuals cannot be divorced from their physical, narrative and historical contexts. All choreographic material is a narration and, therefore, should convey some kind of message. At the same time, all *danse nouvelle* choreographers drew their distinctive narrative styles from a variety of backgrounds and international tendencies, particularly from such different schools as French *danse académique*, American abstract postmodern dance, German *tanztheater* and Japanese *butoh*, as well as contemporary theater, especially the absurdist theater of Beckett and Ionesco.

Choreographically, Marin created her first piece in 1976, called *Yu-Kuri*, for Bejart's *Ballet du XX Siècle*, where she had been dancing since 1972. Nevertheless, her choreographic career began in 1977 when, after leaving Bèjart, Marin conceived a piece for her own company, the *Ballet Thêâtre de l'Arche*, created in collaboration with Daniel Ambash. Her first work, *Evocation*, premiered in the Nyon International Competition in Switzerland and won a first prize. She has been continuously productive as a choreographer since then.

Maguy Marin is also one of the most financially stable artists of the new generation. Favored by the new cultural policies of the French government with the objective of improving the nation's artistic scene, she has been officially settled in Créteil, a small town outside Paris, since 1983. There she annually creates State-sponsored pieces for the *Companie Maguy Marin* (ex-*Ballet Thêâtre de L'Arche*). She also works as an invited choreographer for such companies as the Lyon Opera Ballet, the Paris Opera, the Nancy Opera and the Dutch National Ballet.

Marin's choreographic style relies on dramatic dance-theater pieces, where painstakingly crafted *tableaux vivants* conjure movement, as well as visual images and sounds. All her creations, although varied in thematic and formal terms, reveal a consistent preoccupation with the drama of human nature. The Biblicaly inspired *Babel, Babel* and *Eden* and the fairy-tale-based *Cendrillon* project views of lost innocence. The Beckettian *May B* presents solitary and hopeless men, frustrated in their social and political projects. *Calambre* denounces Spanish culture, shadowed by the shames of the past and *Qu'est-ce que ç'a fait a moi?* sarcastically looks at the Bicentennial of the French Revolution.

Despite her concerns with meaning, however, Marin's narratives are never linear or straightforward. In her spectacular theatrical pieces, the movement, even when derived from the balletic vocabulary, is not the main focus. Following a general tendency of European dance, Marin's choreography is totally free in its abundant use of theatrical elements. Dancers interact equally with music, text, props, sets, light and costumes, and all elements serve as instruments to communicate the choreographer's ideas and concerns. Dance is narrative drama told by means of integrated elements in and outside the dance medium.

Breaking the narratives through fragmentation, Marin radically inserts films, songs or dialogues into her works. Within a multimedia universe set onstage, Marin creates poignant worlds. Her pieces depend as much on the assertion of their physical, spatial and formal immediacy as upon cultural context and intellectual references. The strength of her narratives emanates from the thematic sources and from the various relationships established among movement and visual and sound information. In that sense, Marin's dances parallels the "theater of images" of Robert Wilson.

Here it seems appropriate to highlight an important difference between Maguy Marin and the German choreographer Pina Bausch, with whom Marin is often compared. While Bausch's pieces are shaped from primary material in the form of raw, distilled emotional states, Marin conveys her works through visual ideas, where images, movement and sound relate to specific preconceived themes. Marin has formalist concerns that are based on her quest for *how* to convey narrative (Marin, personal interview, 1990).

A Toysh Cinderella

In 1984, Maguy Marin had to face a difficult task: she was invited to recreate *Cinderella* for the Lyon Opera. The challenge was not only to recreate a fairy tale which had been staged so many times in the ballet tradition, but also to work within an idiom which Marin had abandoned since she left the Strasbourg Opera in 1968, seeing it as "elitist and aristocratic" (Marin, personal interview, 1990). The crisis in French society provoked by the 1968 student upheaval reinforced her refusal to "create classicism for the rich bourgeoisie."

What about *Cinderella*? How would Marin approach a choreography designed for a ballet company? Maguy Marin certainly knew the *Cinderella* story through its Charles Perrault and Walt Disney versions, and she had harsh opinions about them:

> To me, fairy tales are something reserved for childhood...I was never really in touch with fairy tales because they did not fit with the kind of stark background I received. In my childhood, I used to be very angry with these stories where every poor, little girl was always saved by a rich person, usually the fragile girl rescued by a sumptuous prince. Money was always a redemptory factor in fairy tales (personal interview, 1990).

There is a direct line from Perrault in the seventeenth century to the Walt Disney contemporary filmic version, as they both have used fairy tales as models to set standards for civilization directed to upper-class children (Zipes, *Art of Subversion*). Fairy tales are specially directed to girls and women, who were at the center of Perrault's reflections. In his collections, Perrault chose tales which showed the "ideal virtues" of a woman, namely beauty, sweetness, kindness, obedience to the husband, dedication to the maintenance of the home, loyalty and lack of coquetry (31).

As the majority of literary fairy tales have female protagonists, and most of them are saved by men, these stories have turned into models of behavior for girls. In "Things Walt Disney Never Told Us," Kay Stone reminds us that, while she wears dirty rags, Cinderella has to conceal herself completely. She can only become a heroine after she is cleaned and dressed (44). And, of course, when she is covered with gold and jewels.

At the time of the choreography, Maguy Marin had read Bruno Bettelheim's *The Uses of Enchantment: The Meaning and Importance of Fairy Tales*, which provides a psychoanalytical analysis of the tale, relating it to sibling rivalry and sexual emancipation. Nevertheless, she asserted that she was not interested in entering the realms of questioning its meaning. Limiting the fairy tale to realms exclusively belonging to children, Marin affirmed that she was not concerned with what the story meant, but she was rather focused on how to tell the children's story—how to build her own spectacle maintaining the canonical Perrault's *Cinderella* version.

Nevertheless, her affirmation raises important questions about the construction of meaning in performance. The choreographer said she was not interested in changing the tale's meaning and thus maintained the narrative as it was written by Perrault, but meaning in performance is not only embodied through textual narrative. Through visual, sound and kinetic elements, Marin has, in fact, consistently subverted the meaning of the story. Or, at least, she has subverted the mythicized, classical point of view through which we see *Cinderella* as depicted by Perrault and Walt Disney, as well as in the ballet tradition from Didelot to Petipa and his followers.

Cinderella is probably the most popular fairy tale in the world and the generic Cinderella-type tales is one of the first narratives to appear within the tradition of storytelling (Opic and Opie 152). As Alan Dundes had shown in his *Cinderella: A Casebook*, there are thousands of Cinderella tale types registered in Italy, Scotland, Scandinavia, Germany, France, Egypt, China, Africa, and the Americas. The consistent theme tells of a girl who is mistreated by her stepmother. As she receives some kind of magical help—most of the time it comes from her dead mother—the girl gets access to a special, luxury or ritualist occasion. She hides herself, later goes back to her life of poverty and suffering and in her rush back home, forgets one of her shoes. The shoe is found by a prince who had been charmed by her mysterious presence. After trying it on every possible woman, he finds her and they marry.

Iona and Peter Opie tell about the tale type shown in a Chinese book dated about 850-860 A. D., which is probably the first one to be recorded in writing. In this tale, collected by a man named Tuan Ch'eng-shih, the heroine, Yeh-hsien, suffers the same injustices from her stepmother and sister and secretly (for her own decision) goes to a festival with a cloak of kingfisher feathers and shoes of gold, immediately charming the ruler of the kingdom. As, at the end, the shoe fits her foot and she marries the king, the stepmother and stepsister are independently killed by flying stones.

Jack Zipes discusses the possible matriarchal origins of this tale, quoting the work of German scholars August Nitschke and Heide Gottner-Abendroth, where it is said that the oral tale of *Cinderella* is traced back to matrilineal societies where the gift-bearing mother, who is dead, gives her daughter three gifts that enable her to complete tasks in the underworld, sea and sky so that she can liberate a man, who is in a beastly state. Rescued and humanized by the girl, the man integrates himself into a tribe governed by matrilineal rites of goddess (*The Brothers Grimm*, 137).

Zipes describes an oral tale that is a *Cinderella* tale variant, told among Muslim women and recorded by anthropologist Margaret A. Mills (qtd. in Dundes *Cinderella*, 180-192). The tale reveals a strong affinity to matrilineal moon worship. Here the girl Mahpishani, whose dead mother is substituted by an evil teacher, is guided by her gift-bearing dead mother who is transformed into a cow. With her help, the girl completes various tasks successfully and is rewarded with the sign of the moon and the stars marked in her body. Men are incidental, as the father and the prince are passive prizes of the women's struggle. They are simply male brides.

The *Cinderella* tale has in fact marks of matriarchal lineage, which were nevertheless obfuscated because of society's patriarchalization, during the course of four millennia, approximately from 7000 B.C. to 3000 B. C.. At that time, oral tales with female protagonists and rituals celebrating the moon goddess were gradually substituted by stories emphasizing male superiority and sun-worshiping rituals (*The Brothers Grimm*, 141).

In their later, literary versions, fairy tales have continuously reinforced patriarchalization. To write his *Cinderella or the Glass Slipper* in the seventeenth century, Charles Perrault used Giambattista Basile's *La Gatta Cenerentola*, a story included in his *Pentamerone* collection. There the heroine named Zezolla maintains some traces of the orally propagated matrilineal tradition.

Zezolla is the only daughter of a prince who marries for the second time a woman whom she dislikes. She thus plots with her governess to murder her stepmother, so the latter can take over as the new prince's wife. After breaking the woman's neck, Zezolla realizes her mistake. The ex-governess turns out to be much worse than the former wife, placing her six daughters over her and mistreating her constantly. Zezolla's milieu becomes the kitchen and she becomes known as the gatta cenerentola (the hearth-cat).

At the time of a *festa*, Zezolla is helped by a magical date tree, which can be seen as a symbolical representation of her dead mother. The tree, that had grown of the size of a woman, provides her with clothing and horses for the ball, where she goes three times, with the condition that she keeps herself unrecognized by the stepmother and sisters. Needless to say, the king falls in love with the stranger, she runs away and, in her anxiety, during the third day, she drops a beautiful shoe that the king eventually tries on all the ladies of the kingdom. At the end, after the stepsisters have tried to cut their toes off to try to fit the shoe, Zezolla is the one who succeeds naturally and becomes the Queen.

Perrault took this tale and reworked it according to the *preciosité* rules of the baroque period and the lessons of virtue and high education that he wanted to imprint on the story. The author is indeed responsible for the theme of the cinder-girl who is only able to attend a ball by the benevolence of a fairy godmother, on condition that she returns before midnight (Opie and Opie), as well as the legendary image of the glass slipper as a perfect symbol of aristocratic refinement, that eventually became classical or "mythicized" in the Western fairy tale tradition.

In contrast to Perrault's heavy patriarchalization of *Cinderella* — an approach later reinforced in Walt Disney's filmic version — the nineteenth-century version written by the Grimms was more faithful to Basile's and kept some residues of matriarchal themes. The Brothers' Cinderella gets her magical help from a tree planted from seeds given by her father as a gift from a trip.

Differently from Basile's, the Grimms' version does not contain radical brutal acts such as the breaking of the step-mother's neck. However, violence recurrently appears in the Grimms' version. For example, in order to try to fit the shoe on their feet, the two stepsisters also cut their toes off and the bleeding is clearly stated. At Cinderella's wedding with the

prince, birds come and eat the eyes of the stepsisters who were
serving as bridesmaids, making them blind.

Perrault's French baroque tradition praised aristocratic
good manners and unconditional forgiveness over the Grimms
more real life cruel punishments. The French author, more
than any other fairy tale writer, was able to transform Cinderella, from an active girl who has to struggle to regain her
social rights after her mother's death, into a pretty, passive
and unconditionally good lady (Zipes, *Art of Subversion* 30).
And it was mostly from her French tradition that Marin drew
her playful yet critical comment on the Cinderella tale, as will
be seen further.

Created for a ballet company, Maguy Marin's *Cinderella* also
follows a long line of other ballet productions. Nevertheless,
the expectation of a traditional ballet performance in Marin's
piece is initially cut off by the presence of a huge dollhouse
covering the stage space and by the transformation of the
dancers' bodies, padded and dressed in cartoonish costumes,
their heads covered by large doll-like masks.

In other *Cinderella* ballets, and perhaps in most narrative
ballets, the story is almost an excuse for moments of pure
dancing, and the characters' emotions are nicely aestheticized
through pantomime which advances the plot. To prevent the
Lyon ballet dancers from using mimetic expressions which
they were used to, Marin had them wear masks. The masks
were eventually expanded into full dolls and framed the performance with all the apparatus of fantasy associated with
infancy. Marin wanted the dancers to look like old wax dolls,
with very large heads, out of proportion to the bodies. These
masks refracted peripheral vision, hampering the dancers'
movements and giving them a clumsy appearance.

Marin's main fear was that she would be tempted to sacrifice
her own choreographic visions to the balletic conventions,
especially since she knew she was to use Prokofiev's musical
score. She thus initially decided to cut off some musical pieces
which she found too explicitly dramatic—from fifty original
musical pieces, she used thirty five. She eventually included an
original sound composition created by composer Jean
Schwarz, mixing baby babbling, electronic growls, and mur-

murs. Throughout the dance, Marin aimed to maintain a childhood sensibility, imprinting the balletic choreography with a movement quality which was simple, mostly angular and deliberately clumsy, often marked by children's game motifs. Finally, limiting the space in order to avoid grandiose balletic jumps and turns, and following the childhood theme, Marin envisioned a three-stage dollhouse set to occupy the stage space. The dollhouse contains nine compartments, and is initially wrapped in translucent plastic until lighting spots illuminate "rooms," as the dancers move up and down in it. This set provides the stage with a specific spatial frame and perspective and also introduces the spectator, even prior to the performance, to the choreographer's particular view of the fairy tale.

In contrast to other story ballet productions, which are structured within modes alternating imitation (mimetic gestures to advance the plot) and the display of pure dancing, Marin's movement construction narrates the *Cinderella* tale through its own theatricality. The clarity of dynamics and shapes; the simplicity of motifs, often repeated to build the characters' identities in the story; and the overall didactic quality of the movement based on the balletic code are reminiscent of the German masterpiece *The Green Table,* choreographed by Kurt Jooss in 1932. Like the German work, Marin's *Cinderella* plays with notions of innovation and tradition, blurring the lines between the avant-garde and the old-fashioned.

In *Cinderella*, Marin has created movements which directly revisit the way automaton dolls move. These gestures are marked by angularity and stiffness, produced by a predominant use the peripheral parts of the body. In addition, the movements occasionally invoke generic qualities of childhood, qualities replicated, for example, in the performers' demonstration of insecurity to perform the steps or, at other times, an exuberant spontaneity. The choreographer also makes use of mimetic movements whenever she directly quotes specific children's games. For example, when playing with fairies and animals before going to the ball, Cinderella rolls with them on the floor, doing somersaults and playing leap frog with them.

Each of the dancers has a movement style directly related to the character (s)he represents. The stepsisters and stepmother are fat, bad and overconfident and they move heavily, with bent knees. Cinderella has more delicate yet still childish gestures revealing a dreamy and tentative personality. When she is ready to go to the ball, she rehearses ballet steps but she keeps falling down all the time. She has to roll over to push herself up; she moves with the rigidity and unpredictability of an infant taking her first steps. Her falls are metonymic of her own purity.

Marin's vocabulary is coined from the ballet lexicon. Nevertheless, the choreographer has cleared it of its stylistic ornamentation, like those of the *port de bras* and their accompanying head positions. She has turned the romantic idealizations of the prototypical ballet dancer's body, gracious and full of flowing poses, into doll and cartoon-like ones. Cinderella's masked face and slightly stuffed upper body — a device designed to cover up the dancer's breasts so she could impersonate a child — forces us to see her movement differently. She cannot be a pretty young woman doing pretty dancing, as we would expect from the heroine of a typical fairy tale ballet.

At the same time, presenting dolls moving to well-defined balletic steps, Marin is playing with notions of expectation and convention. The result is awkwardly funny as we see, for example, a duet of Cinderella and the prince, two naive dolls engaged in a reverential dance, where ballet steps interweave with childish clapping of approval directed at each other. In lieu of romantic arabesques with the male dancer supporting the ballerina, Marin presents unexpected *pas-de-deux* moves, like one where Cinderella climbs on the prince's knees and sits on his shoulders.

Syntactically, the dance is organized in three parts: the first one shows Cinderella at home; the second, at the ball; and the third depicts the protagonist at home again. The first part of the dance introduces the characters: Cinderella, the stepmother and the sisters, the father and the fairygodmother. Each of these characters has a specific way of moving in space, and their particularities are demonstrated through interactions, within group dances. For instance, in the beginning, we understand who the stepsisters are by the way they interact and contrast with Cinderella, throwing her from one to the other, pushing her away and pointing at her face, while the protagonist keeps a much lighter gestural style.

The ball presents the court members, who are extensions of the stepmother and sisters *personae*, both in their movement style and in their looks. The court members dance in mirroring group movements, reminiscent of a typical baroque minuet. The ball also delineates the romance between the prince and Cinderella, which is embodied through playful duets. The third part begins with Cinderella's opening solo and is climaxed by a later romantic duet between Cinderella and the prince.

Narrative Structures

A comparison between Perrault's narrative tale and Marin's dance *Cinderella* will give insights of the significance of this recreation. Following Propp's classification, Charles Perrault's literary *Cinderella* (AT 510A and KHM 21), first published in 1692, could be separated into the following functions:

(α) *Initial situation.* Perrault's introduces the hero, talking about the death of Cinderella's mother and the father's remarriage. He also introduces the ugly and bad stepmother and stepsisters.

(A) *Villainy.* In Perrault, this corresponds to the ill-treatment that the stepmother and sisters dispense to Cinderella, putting her to work in the house and making her live by the ashes, while they have a good and luxurious life.

(γ) *Interdiction.* Cinderella cannot go to the royal ball like her stepsisters, since she is so poor and dirty. She is nevertheless so good that she helps her sisters with their clothes and hairdos.

(B⁷) *Lament or cry for help.* As the sisters leave for the ball, Cinderella begins to cry.

(F⁶/⁹) The meeting with a helper. Her fairy godmother suddenly appears, asking her why she is crying and offering her magical services.

(D¹) The helper's tasks for the hero. As Cinderella explains that she would love to go to the ball but has no means to do it, the fairygodmother asks Cinderella to bring her a pumpkin, a mouse, a rat, and lizards, to be transformed by her into the coach, the horses and the coachman. This part includes the attribute (99) which relates to the gold and the jewels of Cinderella's outfit and also the shoe made of crystal, a deliberate invention of Perrault reinforcing the delicacy by which Cinderella had to move and behave in order not to break it (Zipes, *The Brothers Grimm* 146). The last task refers to the fairygodmother's command that Cinderella return before midnight, which was also set by Perrault as a moral lesson for well-behaved girls.

(G) Transference to the ball. The hero, Cinderella is conducted in a marvellous golden coach headed by six footmen, six horses and a coachman.

(H²) The place of confrontation with the villain: the ball. Upon being informed that a 'grand princess' had arrived whom nobody knew, the king's son went forth to greet her. The guests stopped dancing, so impressed they were with her beauty. All the ladies were busy examining her headdress and golden clothes because they wanted to obtain some similar garments the next day.

(I²) Victory without battle. Cinderella gained the prince's love and attention. He could not take his eyes away from her. Besides her beauty, Cinderella's conduct during the ball was exemplary. Perrault uses the occasion to teach lessons of *civilité* writing that, during the supper, Cinderella "showed her sisters a thousand civilities, as she shared with them oranges and citrons that the prince had given her" (Zipes, *Beauties* 25-27). As the clock shows a quarter to midnight, Cinderella returns home before her stepmother and sisters.

(*J*²) *Transference of a lost object.* In the next evening, she goes back to the ball, dressed even more splendidly than before. This time, however, she is so entertained dancing with the prince that she forgets about the time. As the clock sounds midnight, she starts running away as fast as she can. She drops one of her glass slippers, which the prince catches, promising himself to marry whoever fits it.

(*0*) *Unrecognized arrival.* Cinderella is back home and dressed in rags again after she ran out of the ball. Everybody in the court hears about the prince's intention to marry the lady who fits the slipper, and the stepsisters are excited about the possibility of becoming princesses.

(*L*) *Claims of the false heroes.* As the prince goes to Cinderella's house, the stepsisters try the shoe on. Here, Perrault has eliminated Basile's preceding version in *La Gatta Cenerentola* (used later by the Grimms) which includes the mutilation of the feet by the stepsisters in order to fit the slipper (Bettelheim 251).

(*Q*) *Recognition of the true hero.* Cinderella timidly asks her sisters to let her try the shoe on. They ridicule her but accept it and, much to their surprise, Cinderella's foot easily fits the shoe.

(*U [neg.]*) *The false heroes are not punished for what they had done.* Cinderella immediately pardons the stepsisters for the evil they have caused her and tells them that she wants them to always love her.

(*W**) *Marriage and accession to the throne.* The excessively good Cinderella even marries the stepsisters to two gentlemen of the court.

(α) Marin's choreographic version shows Cinderella leaning over a broom and then sweeping the floor with it. She wears white tights and a plain brown apron. Her hair is long, straight and pink and her mask has an innocent expression, as if nothing had been written on her face.

Marin's Cinderella doll slides her hand on her forehead, demonstrating that she is tired, but there is no explicit reference to her ill-treatment and dirty conditions, no references to her familial background, or even the (γ) to go to the ball. There is neither any demonstration of (B^7).

An act of (A) is only indirectly suggested by the appearance of the stepsisters and stepmother and their movement quality in relation to Cinderella's. The crudely stuffed stepsisters and stepmother have masks which are aged, wrinkled baby faces, rounded and marked by angry expressions, and their hair-pieces are green and yellow mops. They wear the same black boots and laced-skirts and their movements are angular and grotesque. They are bulldozers, pushy and rudely overconfident as they place their hands on their waists and point at Cinderella, with their hips stretched to the opposite direction, as if despising and making fun of her.

The $(F^{6/9})$ function does not derive from a cry for help with the appearance of the fairy godmother, coming out of nowhere, as in the Perrault tale. Here, Marin seems to have coined ideas from other versions of the tale, specially that of the Grimms, first written in 1812. In this literary version, as the father travels, he asks the three sisters what they want him to bring them. Cinderella, instead of gifts, asks for a hazel branch. She plants it on her mother's grave and when it becomes a tree, a white bird which flies around it provides her with magical help (Bettelheim 251-256).

The choreographer combined the gift idea with Perrault's fairy godmother figure. The scene begins with the father arriving with two big gift boxes and a suitcase. After the two sisters avidly pick up each of the gift boxes, Cinderella kisses her father languidly and carries his suitcase. As she is left alone on the stage, an enormous and soft white, gurgling rag doll magically comes out of the suitcase scaring Cinderella. As soon as she starts stretching the doll's limbs, the rag doll "grows" and starts growling, a loud sound reminiscent of a monster's, perhaps echoing Cinderella's own fear of the apparition. She eventually overcomes the fear and responds to the doll with gaga baby noises. She then pulls herself inside the open suitcase, hugs the doll and starts rolling it outside and playing with it. They become like two children relating to one another with rolling movements.

As the rag doll stretches and curls accompanied by a machinery sound, the cloth covering its body unravels, revealing the image of a robot-like figure—this transformation after Cinderella's warm contact is as a reference to popular seventeenth-century French "beauty and the beast" fairy tale motifs. Here, physical appearance is transformed by means of love, trust and virtue.

Marin has chosen to create a slick, androgynous and mechanized fairy, both because she thinks that "fairies, like angels have no sex" and because she sees extraterrestrial, futuristic creatures as a direct, contemporary transposition of the romantic otherworldly quality of fairies, nymphs and sylphs (Marin, personal interview, June 1990). The fairy is bald, wears a white suit, which is like a military uniform, full of small blinking lights and carries a sword, in place of a wand, making staccato fencing poses with it.

Both the glass slipper and the idea of transforming objects such as the pumpkin and the mice into a coach and horsemen were deliberately created by Perrault, who metaphorically idealized the transformation of the mundane into the aristocratic (Bettelheim 261). In the dance, tasks for the hero, and the attribute 99—gold and jewels related to Cinderella's dress and coach—are altogether abandoned.

The fairy simply blesses Cinderella with the sword and points to a window display from which two futuristic fairies, reminiscent of Osckar Schlemmer's Triadic Ballet dancers, dressed in black-and-purple, appear. They show a small convertible toy car and a model holding an austere short pink crinoline skirt. The fairy takes a pair of red dancing shoes, with his/her sword and gives them to Cinderella. These are all the tools that Cinderella needs to go to the ball. There is no need for opulent, baroque-like, gold embroidered outfits of Perrault's story. Or for crystal slippers, symbolic of the extreme refinement of baroque court women. Abandoning the measurements of social status associated with baroque luxury, Marin has created a political statement: Cinderella's attractiveness relies on her simplicity and spontaneity, not on money.

In *(G)*, Cinderella is not conducted to the ball on her coach, but she drives herself in a miniature car. Here the choreographer has undoubtedly given the passive Cinderella as depicted by Perrault and Walt Disney a more active behavior, which revisits her original personality derived from matrilineal societies, and was maintained, for example, in Basile's tale of Zezolla.

(H²) interweaves group movements reminiscent of baroque court minuets with successions of children's games and a duet between Cinderella and the prince. Marin has turned the ball into a typical children's birthday celebration: the prince blows the candles of a decorated cake, his guests receive mint sticks and lollypops, and everyone plays games.

The scene starts with a parade by a crowd of court members, including the stepsisters and mother, packed on the top of the dollhouse's stairs. The court members share with the stepsisters a padded look, and their movements follow a stereotyped, grotesque manner, reminiscent of cartoon-like characters. They come down the stairs seated, bumping from step to step, following the prince who walks alone, stepping slowly and delicately.

The prince shares with Cinderella a less stereotyped look. He wears a grey suit and his mask depicts a gentle facial expression. He has straight blue hair and a crown made up of small blinking lights. When arriving at the ground floor, the group applauds the prince who sits on his throne, a baby chair.

One door slowly opens, and under a curtain of pink smoke, Cinderella arrives driving her car. The prince comes close and kisses her hand. He and Cinderella start a lyric duet where each one touches the other timidly and carefully and then steps back, frightened. As they come forward and then step backwards from one another, advancing slowly each time, they recreate a naturally evolving process of trusting, love and friendship.

In front of them, in two parallel lines, the court members make gestures of surprise as they again perform a kind of baroque minuet. They later start to interact with Cinderella and the prince, as if wanting to dance with them. In the middle of this crowd, Cinderella and the prince start to walk backwards, slowly escaping from the crowd and they end up by touching back to back. While they hug, the court members come walking towards them making gestures of gossip and surprise. A loud children's murmur starts. Cinderella and the prince become frozen, like statuettes, and they are manipulated by the court members, who place them together in an embraced pose. Here Marin may be commenting on the passivity of fairy tale heroes, and the social and ideological pressures that build these expectations.

In (I^2), Cinderella does not gain the prince's attention for her splendorous beauty. Her victory comes from the slow process of mutual discovery, punctuated by courtesy and children's games. Marin has given initiative to her protagonist, in accordance with the original Cinderella type heroine, who was anything but passive.

In Marin's ball, Cinderella takes the initiative of touching the prince's hand, while in response, he gives her a lollypop. They bow toward each other and start a playful and romantic *pas-de-deux*. They both perform the same sliding movements, mirroring each other: They bend and stretch their bodies, curving their torsos in a circled movement, interweaving these movements with hugging and bowing towards each other. It is a balanced duet, with no dominating figure. Here the male figure is given no manipulative powers as in traditional classical ballet forms. The two dancers finally separate and wave at each other, each one kissing the palms of his/her own hands and sending kisses. They relate with the freedom and spontaneity of children not watched by adults. Creating a balanced pas de deux which is performed by two masked dolls, Marin could be making a statement of skepticism: lack of dominance is only possible in a world of dolls and childhood.

Societal tasks and rituals, including a fight of good (Cinderella and the prince) versus evil (the court members including the stepsisters), were added to the ball scene and translated through children's games. The court members appear from an upper room, climbing downstairs with a birthday cake and candles to be blown out by the prince. They come toward him and make ominous faces at Cinderella. Others draw with chalk on the floor and make the prince play hop scotch. They forcefully carry the prince away from Cinderella pulling his ears toward the game place, manipulating his legs in order to step while Cinderella, observing him from the front, imitates his gestures as if hoping that he will perform them correctly. Others prepare the jump rope for Cinderella, who goes under it and starts to learn how to jump. The rope holders increase its speed until it is so fast that Cinderella falls down.

Through the ominous faces and challenges, Marin presents a naive, stock vision of good and evil. The prince comes and helps her stand up. They finally caress each other, victorious, and start to dance until the clock sounds midnight.

(J^2) occurs initially in a manner parallel to that of Perrault's story. At the sound of the clock which points to midnight the robot-fairy appears, and, holding a sword upwards, freezes the whole scene. Only Cinderella has mobility as she slides and rolls down the steps and leaves—her shoe slides off her foot. Different from Perrault's version, where a gentleman is sent to look for the girl who fits the shoe, Marin has the prince himself look for her as he rides a wood toy horse against a backcloth with a stylized landscaped painted on it. He is followed by a line of court members, futuristic fairies and little men and animals all carrying toys such as small airplanes.

(*L*) is symbolically represented with a Flamenco and a belly dancer trying the shoe on. These characters do not exist in the Perrault's literary fairy tale, but were popularized in the Petipa ballet versions of *Cinderella* and *The Nutcracker*, representing stereotypical and exotic ways of dancing as *divertissement*.

The Flamenco and belly dancer solos have a witty, and funny tone as they present a awkwardly doll-like, caricatured version of seduction. The one represented by the Flamenco dancer is aggressive, like a *femme fatale* with angular, large and stretched movements; the other, embodied by the belly dancer is compliant, docile and passive and is based on rounded, fluid and organic movements.

The Flamenco dancer wears a bright yellow dress with black pom-poms and has her long dark hair covered with flowers. She plays the castanets and continuously stretches her legs upwards, one at a time, using them to cling to the prince's body. She tries on the shoe, as she is lying down with her leg pointed straight up. But the shoe does not fit. Nonetheless, she still tries to seduce the prince with her dance and her dramatic arm gestures, but he steps backwards avoiding her. She finally leaves behind a frame reminiscent of a typical Andalucian balcony, full of flowery ceramic vases, carried away from the stage by the doll-animals.

The prince then rides his wood horse again and stops in front of an Arab belly dancer who is sitting on a rug. Her masked face, presenting a placid expression, is framed by a long white tulle and her rounded bustier is silver metallic. She stands up while performing rounded gestures with her arms and shaking her hips, circling them in the air. The animals carry her upwards and the prince then tries the shoe on her foot. As it does not fit, the animals carry her back to the floor over the rug, taking her away, while her hands draw circles on her face, reproducing a passive and languid crying.

In *(O)*, the lights focus on Cinderella's house where she is leaning over the broom and sweeping the floor, in a scene which repeats the beginning of the dance. Different from Perrault's passive heroine, Marin has made her Cinderella a resourceful, good-humored and creative person. She plays with a broom, laying it over a chair and wrapping it with a cloth. She places a smaller chair on its side and sits on it, playing with the broom as if it were her friend or lover—possibly the prince. But as the stepmother and the two sisters arrive, Cinderella immediately puts the chairs away, scared.

The traditional *(L)* function presents the stepsisters trying on the shoe. As the prince arrives, the three sit on other chairs frowning at Cinderella. The way they forbid Cinderella to try the shoe is literal and cartoonish: the stepmother sits on Cinderella, hiding her under her legs. The two stepsisters come running in his direction and take clumsy poses. The prince tries to fit the shoe on their feet unsuccessfully and is about to leave when the fairy points the sword up again.

(Q) is also literal: with the magical help of the robot-fairy pointing his/her sword towards her, Cinderella acquires great strength and is able to push the stepmother's legs away from her. She stands up, sits on a chair and fits the shoe on her foot while taking the other shoe from her apron and wearing it. She and the prince then hug each other, and at this point a baby growl sound replaces Prokofiev's music.

(Ex) and (U) are different from those of Perrault's. Cinderella does not forgive the stepsisters or even hug them like Perrault's Cinderella does. Nor is there an overdramatic and violent ending, as in the Brothers Grimm version where birds eat the stepsisters and mother's eyes. In Marin's ballet, the stepmother and stepsisters are punished by three little men who tie them to their chairs with thick ropes. They leave the stage packed together, jumping and making ugly faces while seated.

(W*) is symbolically performed as the fairy points the sword towards the couple, "blessing" them. Cinderella and the prince kiss and engage in a sweet duet until the scene freezes and people start to slowly leave the stage. A kind of royal heritage is schematized by a final scene where everyone walks crossing the stage, each one pulling different toys on their hands. Cinderella and the prince walk together hand-in-hand, carrying a huge toy which is a never ending line of rubber baby dolls representing their babies. This lyrical but stock ending may represent Marin's skeptical view of fairy tales' classical happy endings.

Parody is Marin's main strategy in this *Cinderella*. The concept of parody here relates to cultural theorist Linda Hutcheon's definition of parody as "repetition with critical distance that allows ironic signaling of difference at the very heart of similarity" (1986: 185). Ballet is still ballet; the Cinderella story is still the story as written by Charles Perrault. Nevertheless, Marin's *Cinderella* has a different ideology and thus subverts its own source.

In her rereading of *Cinderella*, Marin is still offering us a happy ever-after ending, with a perverse stepmother and sisters, a good fairygodmother and a passionate prince. She is even giving us a recognizable lexicon made of ballet steps. Nevertheless, the way these elements are arranged and parodied in the performance context, reinterprets and changes the story's perspective.

Hutcheon explains that the postmodern parody leads to a vision of interconnectedness between innovation and convention, past and present, as it incorporates and modifies past references, giving them new life and meaning and illuminating the work in relation to its sociological situation. She asserts that everything presented and received through language is loaded with meaning. Nevertheless, the mass culture homogenizes meaning, emptying it of its original context. Postmodern parody tries to confront this uniformization and commodification by asserting ironic differences instead of either homogeneous identity or alienated otherness. Parody is thus a mechanism that challenges our homogenizing social notions of the monolithic—male, Anlgo, white, Western (183-184).

By giving us clues of pre-existing *Cinderella* versions through the narrative line and the use of balletic conventions, and turning it into a doll story, Marin is constructing a double parody. First, she is parodying the tale of a seventeenth century rich bourgeois belonging to the baroque court of Louis XIV (Perrault), who adapted a folk tale into a literary story of a princess-to-be, so he could teach moralizing and civilizing lessons directed to upper-class women. Second, by her use of ballet steps, Prokofiev's score, and even the balletic characters of the Flamenco and the belly dancer, Marin is parodying romantic notions of classical ballet, where narrative is aestheticized and sketchy, becoming an excuse for the display of virtuosic technique and the presentation of the ideal woman: the light, delicate and flexible ballerina.

Marin's instrument for parody is the miniaturization of the characters, who become doll/children inhabiting the dollhouse. This parody is in itself loaded with historical references and conventions, revisiting the French nineteenth-century infatuation with the mechanized dolls, named *automates*.

Literary critic Susan Stewart connects the dollhouse with the discourse of the "petite feminine," a discourse that is closely related to that of the fairy tales, mostly inhabited by passive heroines. Stewart explains that the reduction of physical dimensions results in a multiplication of ideological properties, as the miniature offers a world clearly limited in space but frozen and thereby both particularized and generalized in time. Ideologically it represents wealth, as it presents a myriad of perfect objects, and nostalgia, revisitng a pre-industrial era of miniature toys (61-62).

Framing her dance within the limits of a dollhouse, Marin sets the fairy tale narrative apart from reality. Isolating the story into a boundary of miniaturized artifice, she is expressing a skeptical view towards the traditional models of behavior that these stories have provided for girls.

Similarly it could be said that, when first written in 1695, Perrault's version of *Cinderella* was both signifier and signified (Sassure), as it told the story in itself and, at the same time, embodied concepts and ideas of Louis XIV's court. Nowadays, however, depicting a passive and delicate girl, a world inhabited by princes and court members, and teaching civilizing notions interweaving gold and luxury with unconditional good behavior, Perrault's *Cinderella* has been emptied of its original meaning and its didactic purposes. As it is now, the tale can only be presented as a toyish, miniaturized and anachronic narrative.

In fact, as it privileges group movements among the doll characters, the piece presents *Cinderella* as a collective, toy-like story not to be ever taken as individual reality. Marin is discouraging the Cinderella complex by the very projection of its miniaturized narrative version.

6

Bluebeard As Existential Struggle

Pina Bausch's Fairy Tale

Most scholars agree that *Bluebeard* is a fairy tale probably invented by Charles Perrault, with no direct oral ascendence (Opie and Opie, Bettelheim). The author most likely based his story on the motif of the forbidden chamber, coined from Russian, Scandinavian and other European folktales, and interwove it with a kind of moral lesson that responded to his context and milieu. Perrault wrote *Bluebeard* as a warning message against feminine coquetry, clearly stating the dangers of women's curiosity and disobedience. The *moralité* of the tale advises:

> Curiosity, in spite of its charm,
> Too often causes a great deal of harm.
> A thousand new cases arise each day.
> With due respect, ladies, the thrill is slight,
> For as soon as you're satisfied, it goes away
> And the price one pays is never right
> (trans. Zipes, *Beauties* 35).

To embody this tale, Perrault probably juxtaposed the motif and the *moralité* to the identity of supposedly real Bluebeards, basing his villain on the lifes of two medieval Breton men. They were Comorre de Cursed (500—?) and Gilles de Rais (1404-1440), both popularly known in France for their multiple murders and their repugnant physical appearance. Nevertheless, the historical basis for this connection has never been fully proved (Opie and Opie 134-136).

Although she made use of Perrault's tale as a source, Pina Bausch's *Bluebeard*, first staged in 1977, is harshly different from the French author's story. With Bausch, what is reinforced is not the motif of the forbidden chamber or a moral lesson especially designed for women. Nor is the dramatic action, with the evolution of fairy tale moves from a lack or an act of villainy to a happy *denouement*, following Propp's model. With Bausch, meaning is constantly scrambled and narrative evolution is replaced by long repetitions.

Instead of screening the Manichean differences between good and evil associated with fairy tale narratives, Bausch focuses on the overlapping of emotional states. The choreographer depicts a wide range of nuanced emotions in a violent push-and-pull mode that constantly juxtaposes every emotion with what seems to be its intrinsic contradiction. At the same time, while fairy tales are evolutionary, presenting a conflict and later a resolution where good triumph over evil, Bausch's works are zigzags of fragmented material that do not resolve in a final action.

Pina Bausch draws upon *Bluebeard's* central theme, that of a man who marries a woman and exercises his destructive power over her and reworks it in episodic scenes that parade the most poignant and often ambivalent emotions surrounding the relationship between this man (Bluebeard) and the woman (his wife). Bausch maintains references to the fairy tale source throughout the piece; the most explicit one is a tape recorder playing *Bluebeard's Castle*, the opera based on Perrault by Bela Bartok, which is unceasingly manipulated onstage by the protagonist himself. Despite this reference, the choreographer is not interested in the tale's plot. With Bausch, factual narrative is substituted entirely by the nonsensical narration of emotions. The text gives away to the subtext.

Pina Bausch's choreographic identity responds to her own background and the context of her artistic education. In *A Primer for Pina*, a television special aired by PBS in New York in 1984, Susan Sontag defines Bausch as "an extraordinary innovator whose work expresses emotions in a convulsive style." In trying to summarize the complexity of Bausch's work and performance style, Sontag defines her theatrical material onstage as a result of pre-performance exercises and improvisations where the actors/dancers are often "asked to play themselves."

While Sontag's definitions are not entirely accurate, the writer-philosopher is able to provide some insights about the characteristics of *tanztheater*, the German dance-theater school that launched in the 1970s, paralleling Bausch's own developments as a choreographer. The dance-theater format evolved in Germany from a tradition of expressionist and post-war dance, as well as Bausch's experience both with Kurt Jooss in her native country and her training the United States.

Pina Bausch was born on July 27, 1940, in Solingen, a small city on the edge of the Ruhr industrial district, the daughter of a bar-restaurant owners. Her pastime in a world inhabited by adults was to dance on its tables while watching the idiosyncratic world of the petite bourgeoisie around her. Encouraged by whoever saw her dancing, at age fifteen she began her education at the Folkwang school in Essen, under the direction of Kurt Jooss, the creator of the 1932 expressionist masterpiece *The Green Table*.

Five years later, after receiving a scholarship from the DAAD (German Academic Exchange Service), she went to study in New York. There, at the Julliard School, Bausch studied with Jose Limon, Louis Horst, and Antony Tudor, among others. She became a member of a modern troupe named Dance Company Paul Sanasardo and Donya Feuer and also collaborated with Paul Taylor. Subsequently, in 1961, she was also engaged by the New American Ballet at the Metropolitan Opera House.

Returning to Germany in 1962, Pina Bausch became a soloist of the newly born Kurt Jooss Ballet, where she danced during the six subsequent years. There, Bausch also began to choreograph and, in 1969, she won first prize in Cologne Choreographic Competition with *In the Wind of Time*. At that time, her choreographic talents began to attract attention, which in 1973 resulted in an invitation to become director of the Wuppertal Opera Ballet. In this position, Bausch began choreographing opera-ballets such as *Iphigenea and Taurus* (1974) and *Orpheus and Eurydice* (1975), dance pieces such as *The Rite of Spring* (1975) and a more theatrical work, Brecht/Weil's *The Seven Deadly Sins* (1976). These pieces allowed Bausch's style to evolve, setting the ground for a more multimedia theatrical style that became identified as the German *tanztheater*. The inauguration of *tanztheater* corresponded specifically to the creation of *Bluebeard*. Here, Bausch created for the first time a combination of movement, music and theatrical elements that was neither a ballet nor an opera.

Expressionism, From Ausdrucktanz to Tanztheater

Paralleling the pioneering impulses of American modern dancers, since before the First World War, a generation of German teachers and choreographers including Rudolf von Laban and Mary Wigman, followed by Harald Kreutzberg, Gret Palluca and Kurt Jooss, has sought to free the dance vocabulary from rigid and anachronic balletic codes and create a new type of dance. These artists were attempting to use movement to embody their deepest inner emotions in order to achieve universal laws of expression.

Modern dance in Germany developed mainly from a search for essences that responded to the great anxiety and uneasiness amidst the advent of the First War, as well as Freud's newly discovered psychoanalytical theories. The answer to these realities was a move inwards. For the dancers, as well as for a whole generation of expressionist artists, the only truth would come from inner emotions, since the outer reality proved to be untrustworthy. The other major influences in the shaping of German expressionism came from the Austro-German cabaret tradition, with its desire to transform everyday life into artistic events, and Nietzsche's concept of a "new man".

Nietzsche's work is linked with the origins of modern dance, as he approached the holistic truth of the body expressed through dance. Zarathustra speaks of it directly in a section of *Thus Spake Zarathustra* called "On the Despisers of the Body" (Fraleigh xxxi). And in the same way that Nietzsche's 'new man' would achieve wholeness, being able to undergo the different polarities or ambiguities of reality, the holistic antroposophic movement launched by Rudolf Steiner propagated integration in all aspects of human life, from health to education (Siegel, seminar, 1988).

In dance, this search for the truth and wholeness took different forms, according to the vision of particular choreographers. Rudolf von Laban defended the idea that man must strive to grow beyond everyday existence to achieve a state of *festliches Sein* (active being). This quest led him to create a system of movement—today known as the Effort/Shape method of analysis and a notation system, called *Labanotation*—and the development of the eclectic *Bewegungschore* (movement choirs) where huge groups of untrained dancers, from children to factory workers, were invited to dance and share their place in the universal harmony of movement (Koegler).

Mary Wigman, who was a student of Laban, later developed her own dance, which became known as the *Ausdrucktanz* (literally, the dance of expression). Wigman created solo and group works, where characters were replaced by universal types, generically called Woman, Death, and Pain.. Through her gestures she created allegories functioning as iconographic enlargements of life. Wigman's dance focused on the oscillation of human emotions, as she tried to synthesize opposed poles of tension and relaxation, contraction and expansion. Wigman's *Evening Dances* (1924), for example, condensed the forces of God and Demon within herself.

In searching for a "pure, essential German art," Wigman explored primitive emotional states, expressed in abstract movements using the performers' whole bodies. In doing so, the choreographer created a kind of dance that should impersonate emotion in itself. Within her searches, Wigman choreographed works, like *Totemntanz* (1926) and *Witches Dance* (1929), in which the dancers wore masks. This strategy depersonalized the performers, turning them into universal types and emotions, transcending the boundaries of the material world. They attempted to assume a superhuman stature, echoing Nietzsche's new man (Stewart, Armitage 3-42).

Kurt Jooss, who had been a pupil of both Laban and Wigman and was heavily influenced by them, began to teach and choreograph in ways that separated him from his masters. Jooss belonged to a subsequent historical period and movement in Germany that became known as the *Neue Sachlichkeit*. The concept was coined by curator Gustav F. Hartblaud in

1923, in preparation for a museum exhibition of the works of Otto Dix, George Grosz and other artists who were interested in figurativism and in depicting the social realities of the time.

In spite of being stimulated by the same *zeitgeist* as the expressionists, the *Neue Sachlichkeit* artists created art within a more socially committed spirit. Although the term is more popular within the field of the visual arts, the movement embraced all artistic fields. Playwright Ernst Toller, particularly with his work *Hoopa, wir leben!*, solo performer Valeska Gert, and Jooss participated in it, together with visual artists such as Dix and Grosz (Siegel, seminar, 1988).

Already in 1918, the Dada manifesto had declared that expressionism no longer had anything to do with the efforts made by active people. In the visual arts, the expressionist procedure of capturing inner emotions through brushstrokes had been exhausted. The expressionists saw the world as a whole and sought to reproduce their feelings from the totality of their experience. For the artists of the *Neue Sachlichkeit*, this way of experiencing the world was irretrievably lost. The world revealed itself to be fragmented, broken, and disintegrated.

Historically, the Weimar period was marked by a harsh reality, composed by the restrictions of the Treaty of Versailles over a devastated Germany, the failure of the November Revolution, the great devaluation of the mark, inflation, high unemployment and the seizure of the power by the nazis. Together, these realities already prefigured a second World War, especially after the growing shadows of remilitarization. Indeed, the ascendence of Nazism in Germany had a direct influence in the *Neue Sachlichkeit* artists' disillusions with the expressionist focus on inner emotions while reality was dismantling.

Although Kurt Jooss was strongly influenced by Laban, he did not agree with his master's permissive idea that everyone could be a dancer. Echoing a generalized desire to reorder the world, Jooss created a new dance system, which he called *Eukinetics*. This system was based on Laban's expressionist concepts, but it was embodied within a performance method which valued technique, including balletic postures and steps.

Jooss endorsed the expressionist search for a synthesis of the human experience through art. But to him, this synthesis would come from an ordered fusion of theatrical elements, from dancing to acting into a single performing attitude (Markard).

On the other hand, Jooss did not share the expressionist belief in the redemptive capacity of the artist. While Laban thought that his movement choirs could build a healthier society, the postwar choreographer depicted the hypocrisy and ugliness of a corrupted society through war, death, and prostitution, as if witnessing that the world was not going to be a better place after all the suffering (Tobias). That is what he showed in the ballet *The Green Table*, created in 1932. There, Jooss himself danced the role of an allegorical Death—based on the medieval expressionist figure of the *danse macabre*—meeting people under the circumstances of war, while another group of dancers, depicted as a group of masked, powerful gentlemen, coordinated the destruction that seemed highly profitable to them.

Already in 1927, Jooss had become director of the dance wing of the *Folkwangschule*, an institute catering to the needs of the fine and applied arts. Nevertheless, in 1933, because of his ideas and opposition to Nazism, he went in exile in England. Jooss returned to Essen in 1949, after sixteen years, to regain the position of director. It was there, six years after Jooss's return, that Bausch received her formal education.

However innovative and unique, Pina Bausch's work is undoubtedly rooted in the German expressionist tradition developed in the 1910s and 1920s as well as in a more reality-oriented style based on Kurt Jooss's teachings. Jooss influenced Bausch's use of real-life commentary often inserted in her pieces, which are counterbalanced by expressionist devices such as the search for universal types and emotions. Jooss was also crucial in the shaping of Bausch's multimedia approach to choreography—a combination of visual, musical and kinetic elements in a single piece.

Finally, Bausch additionally learned from her master lessons about "economy of movement." Jooss defended the use of different forms, from old techniques to contemporary performing vocabularies, but only when this was justified. Bausch explains: "Jooss used to say that movement should only be used if it had a significant purpouse for what you want to address; otherwise, you better not do it" (Bausch, personal interview, 1991).

This attitude partially explains the heated polemic among critics involving the classification of Bausch's work. Many American critics refuse to accept Bausch's pieces as dance, since most of the time she does not present performers travelling on the stage in space. In an issue of *The Drama Review* dedicated to German dance, critics Arlene Croce, Marcia B. Siegel, Nancy Goldner, Mindy Aloff, among others, insist on the subservient role that movement plays in Bausch's pieces ("What the Critics Say", Summer 1986, 80-84). In fact, from a merely formal point of view, her work appears to be a theater of images embedded with some kinetic orientation. Nevertheless, as will be discussed further, it is less the appearance and more the logic of its construction that makes Bausch's work undoubtedly connected with dance.

Another important influence in Bausch's style came from American modern dance which she participated during her New York years. The choreographer had close contact with American modern dance with its preoccupation with expression, as in the work of Jose Limon, something prior to the formalist *venue* developed by the Judson postmodern choreographers. Indeed, Bausch main motto differs radically from that of the analytical American post-modern dance choreographers. Bausch is not interested in how people move, but in what moves people. She focuses on expression over form. (Servos 227-230).

Bausch's affirmation is rooted in a generalized reaction against the formalist orientation of German dance after the Second World War, particularly with the revaluing of classical ballet. This happened partially because of the nazist appropriation of *ausdrucktanz*. The nazis put the dance to its ideological service, emptying from its social search of a more unified world and turning it into simple spectacle. This happened, for example, during the 1936 Berlin Olympic Games, where Wigman, Palucca and Kreutzberg choreographed a monumental opening (Kloeger 1974). But above anything, balletic formalism seemed to be a safe refuge in a time of extreme insecurity.

In the sixties, replying against this formalist tendency, Bausch and a generation of other choreographers, including her colleagues in the *Folkwang*, Heinhild Hoffmann and Suzanne Linke, went back to the expressionist traditions of *audrucktanz*, occasionally adding it to the ideas and principles drawn from international experimental theater and American modern dance. Fusing these different techniques, young German choreographers began to call their work *tanztheater* to differentiate it from mainstream *opperballet* (Benson and Manning, *The Drama Review*).

Nevertheless, unlike Jooss and her *audsdructanz* predecessors who would praise simple and stark works, Bausch has always created pieces that are large-scaled, employing a visually rich production style. And, while Jooss is more social oriented, Bausch interweaves the political and the psychological in a mode that constantly shifts between the epic and the personal.

Since directing the Tanztheater Wuppertal in 1973, Bausch has developed the most international and well-known form of *tanztheater*. Although it is subsided by the State, Bausch's Tanztheater Wuppertal is not limited by the demands of local audiences, since the company performs twice as much abroad than it does in its own country. The company's internationality is paralleled inside her multicultural company, composed of dancers from all over the world. Multiculturalism is also expressed within Bausch's pieces, as she often choreographs scenes where the same action, emotion or opinion is repeatedly voiced by each of the performers, who usually give their individual prospectives onstage, expressing them in their own languages (this device was not yet used in *Bluebeard*, which does not have spoken words onstage. Bausch began to make a consistent use of words only after this piece).

Bausch is known for a performance style that is epic, large-scale and spectacular. It is based on repetitions of vignettes that can be composed of gestures, movements, words, music and sounds. These vignettes are repeated, accumulated, transformed and played upon simultaneously with many other things happening onstage. This happens in a fragmentary and juxtaposed fashion that reproduces cinematic or videoclip editings.

Repetition plays a key role in Bausch's work. It reinforces absurd images, stretching its emotional content. As Ann Daly has observed, the effect of repetition in Bausch's work varies from spectator to spectator, as it can either intensify or anesthetize the response to violence. Intensification is brought by an exhaustive accumulation, with the heightening the spectator's sense of anticipation and expectation of violence. Anesthesia may come with the breaking of theatrical surprise provoked by the intense repetition. "That's why some spectators sweat through these sequences while others laugh" (1986:54).

As far as content is concerned, Pina Bausch is mostly absorbed with the disenchantment among human beings; she particularly focuses her attention on the relationship between men and women, which for her seems to be oppressively set and unchangeable: men dominate women; women remain passive. In order to express that relationship, Bausch constantly uses violence to scrutinize emotions such as pain, solitude, compassion and desperation. Dance critic Ann Daly says that in Bausch's pieces repetition is verbatim, as it does not lead to any change. The choreographer ritualizes nihilism in both its physical and emotional aspects ("Tanztheater" 55).

In Bausch's pieces, there is a constant play between representation (theatricality) and reality. Bausch plays with the relationship with the spectator: (s)he feels close to the performance because of the complicity with its psychological and physical impact and because of the pleasure in its rich visual stimuli. On the other hand, (s)he feels detached because different actions start and end without any reason or logic, without any coherent development with which (s)he could relate to.

Although Bausch's style is not *a priori* based on any preconceived theory (personal interview, 1991), it can be related to theatrical techniques created by Stanislavski and Brecht. From the former, she uses the principles of interaction with the intensity and pain of remembered experiences. In the process of creating the pieces, Bausch asks her performers questions of

personal and emotional content, demanding that they impro-
vise scenes based on memories to access what she calls their
"painful zones" (Hoghes).

From Brecht, comes the use of alienation techniques, dis-
missing the spectators' sympathetic identification by presenting their roleplaying as self-consciously theatrical. Brecht's
concept of "epic" indicated a broad mode of performance,
mixing narrative and dramatic techniques that keep the spectator at a certain distance. The notion of *verfremdungseffekt*
(alienation) allows events to be strange enough for the spectator to question them. With Brecht, theatrical elements and
mechanisms are exposed, and narrative becomes episodic in
place of evolutionary, by means of the insertion of songs and
commentary on the scenes (Brecht, *On Alienation*). In Bausch's
pieces, the spectator is engaged in a push and pull mode,
absorbed by the strong emotional impact of the scenes and dis-
tanced by the exhaustive lenght of repetitons. The result is a
lack of resolution (Manning, "American Perspective" 61).

Pina Bausch's *Bluebeard* makes use of Bela Bartok's opera
Duke Bluebeard's Castle, which is the most consistent reference to
the fairy tale in the piece. The music is indeed very crucial for
the organization of the performance and its emotional structure and Bausch's choice of the composer is significant.

Bela Bartok (1881-1945) is considered to have reconciled
the folk melody of his native Hungary with the main currents
of European music. Analogous to the Grimms' expectations
with reproducing the folk—although these expectations were
far from succesful—Bartok intended to translate directly from
the folk, thus capturing universal truths about his cultural
background. The composer went on expeditions to remote
villages of his country to find the spirit of his music. In doing
so, he was driven by a strong nationalist movement that strove
to shake off the domination of Austro-German culture.

Bartok's romantic nationalism attained a climax when Hungary was declared independent of Austria. During that time,
the composer created the music for the ballet *The Wooden
Prince*, a great success at the Budapest Opera, and subsequently, in 1911, the opera *Duke Bluebeard's Castle*. The opera
explores different states of mind, where simple rhythmic struc-

tures are made human by its constant distortions. Bartok's music establishes a connection between the past and the living present, evoking traditions yet keeping its sense of urgency. Bela Bartok's romantic grandiosity was profoundly rooted in his native Hungary, juxtaposing the folk with intellectual erudition. Structurally, his compositions rank with the greatest poignancy, embodying a broad range of human emotions in a synthetic fashion.

Bausch's choice of *Bluebeard* as thematic source relates to her own interest in this story, her desire to "deal not only with the desperation of Judith (the name of Bluebeard's wife given by Bartok), but also the profound solitude of Bluebeard himself" (interview with the author 1991). The choice of Bartok's music is equally understandable by both the familiarity of the choreographer with opera and for her identification with the composer, vis-a-vis their shared interest in condensed, rich emotions.

Narrative Structures

Charles Perrault's *Bluebeard* was adapted by Bela Bartok, who later imprinted changes in the narrative when writing his opera. Bausch has thought of choreographing *Bluebeard*, based both in the idea of the tale as she had known it from fairy tale collections and particularly from Bartok's libretto of *Duke Bluebeard's Castle* (Bausch, personal interview, 1991). Perrault's *Bluebard*, a source for both Bartok and Bausch, can be classified according to Propp, as follows:

(α)*Initial situation*. A man who is as rich as he is ugly — he had a horrible blue beard — proposes the hand of a young lady in marriage. He actually proposes to marry any one of the daughters of a lady of virtue. After cultivating the acquaintance of the family and displaying his fortune and good manners, the lady finally decides to marry him with her youngest daughter.

(W) Wedding. The bride goes to live in his rich palace. At the end of a month after the marriage, Bluebeard tells his wife he

had to take a journey concerning a matter of great consequence, and it would take at least six weeks.

(γ)*Interdiction*. As Bluebeard leaves, he gives his wife the keys
of his palace. They are keys to splendors such as his richest
furniture, gold and silver plates, and caskets of jewels. He tells
her to feel free to invite whoever she wants to divert herself
with during his absence but, nevertheless, forbids her to open
the door of a small closet at the end of the gallery on the
ground floor. He tells her that if she does that, she would
experience his anger in a way that she could not even
imagine.

(↑) *Departure*. As soon as Bluebeard leaves, neighbors and
friends come immediately to see the richness of the place.
They had always been curious about it but were afraid to go
there in the presence of Bluebeard.

(δ′) *Interdiction violated*. While everybody is having a great time
looking around, the wife cannot control her curiosity about
the forbidden closet. She finally cannot resist and, moving in
an excessive haste, impulsively opens the door with the key.

(ϑ^2) *The Hero receives information about the villain*. Terrified, the
woman then sees a bunch of corpses of other women (ex-wives)
and understands that they had been killed by Bluebeard. Desperate, she closes the door after her and runs away.

(θ^2) *The hero falls victim of magical agent*. With horror she realizes
that some blood gets stuck in the key (Perrault explains that
the key is a fairy). She does everything to try to clean it so that
her husband will not discover her disobedience, but when the
blood is gone from one side, it reappears on the other, and so
forth.

(A^{13}) *Villainy/order to kill*. Bluebeard returns home the same
evening of the incident, prior to the predicted date. He immediately asks his wife for the key, which she tries to hide. Eventually, upon his insistence, she gives it to him. Seeing the

bloody key, Bluebeard then cooly tells her that she is going to be killed for her curiosity and lack of loyalty, just as the other women she had seen.

(D$^{5/7}$) Request for mercy and other request. The poor woman implores his forgiveness, but as he stands as inflexible as a stone with the desire to kill her. She then begs for some time, so she can do her prayers upstairs before being killed.

(C) Consent to counteraction. Bluebeard agrees to give her a quarter of an hour, not one second more.

(B^1) Call for help. In a desperate bid to receive help, she asks her sister Anne, who was there in the castle, to go to the top of the tower to see if her brothers (who were supposed to get there at that day) were arriving.

(F^5) Agent/helper is found. After her time has expired, Anne finally sees her brothers arriving. They are two horsemen who enter the castle immediately, carrying their swords — one of them a dragoon, the other a musketeer.

(F^9) Agent/helpers offer services. The brothers arrive at the exact moment when Bluebeard is holding a knife to kill the wife.

(I^1)Victory over the villain in open battle. They quickly pursue him and end up by killing him with their swords.

(W^0) Monetary reward. The woman is now free and rich, having inherited Bluebeard's fortune. She uses one part of it to marry her sister Anne to a young gentleman, another part to buy captains' commissions for her brothers, and the rest to marry herself to a very honest gentleman.

Perrault's message with the *Bluebeard* tale is clear; it is an alert for women to control their curiosity and avoid any possible lack of loyalty vis-a-vis arranged marriages. It was common at that time for women to be victims of forced marriages, and Perrault seemed to be pinpointing to the dangers of breaking marital rules. At the same time, the fairy tale served him to establish a code of good manners, a system of justice and a test for tenderness. As Zipes attests, the brutality and sado-masochism in French fairy tales relate to the fact that morally, the protagonist had to suffer in order to demonstrate his or her nobility and *tendresse* (8).

In *Duke Bluebeard's Castle,* Bela Bartok made some changes to the story. Judith, the young wife, arrives at Duke Bluebeard's magnificent and magical castle. There, she is given the keys to seven doors, the first six to open a torture chamber, an armory, a treasure chamber, a garden of blood, a huge king-dom, and a sea of tears, respectively. She is forbidden to open the seventh door. At her incessant insistence, however, Blue-beard finally opens the chamber, and the murdered corpses of his former wives are shown. In Bartok's more tragic version, Judith recognizes her fate and passively awaits for her own death.

Pina Bausch appropriates the frames of the *Bluebeard* tale and overtly reveals the mechanics of her appropriations. That is why her piece's complete title is *Bluebeard—While Listening to a Tape Recorder of Bela Bartok's Opera "Duke Bluebeard's Castle."* In her reinterpretation, Bausch has transformed Bluebeard, from Bartok's Duke, into a common man, who in the piece is performed by Jan Minark. Blueberad's castle is turned into a stark, old room, with high and closed windows set in murky walls. Beatrice Libonati, a small and tiny dancer, plays his wife, dressed in a poor, simple red dress. It is the manipulation of the tape by Bluebeard/Minark that frames the whole performance.

The stark room, consisting of a chair and a tape deck con-trasts with a monumental floor, all covered with dry leaves. This contrasting device is consistent with Bausch's pieces. Breaking the continuity of an otherwise realistic set, Bausch's pieces present floors often covered with a "tapestry" of some kind of organic (or organic-looking) material, from water, to earth, to leaves, to carnations. This "tapestry" literally sets the ground for the choreographer's hipper realistic mode of rep-resentation and opens the ways for the epic proportions of her work. *Bluebeard's* set covered with leaves is also reminiscent of the fairy tales' enchanted forests, a reference specially consistent with the Germanic quality of the Grimms' fairy tales.

(α) As the piece begins, a man (Bluebeard) is seated in front of a tape recorder, listening to the first bars of the opera. He manipulates the tape, playing and rewinding it continuously, as if trying to search for something in the music. Bluebeard's money, stated in Perrault's story and Bartok's libretto, is here suggested by the image of power presented as he manipulates the tape deck, flipping it on and off, abruptly.

(W) can be inferred by the way he sexually relates to a woman who is laying quietly on the stage floor. He turns the tape off and throws himself on top of her body covered with dried leaves. She tries to drag his weight on top of her by tossing herself, her head flipping jerkily from side to side, until she gives up.

(δ') is symbolically demonstrated in the way the tape is used, playing without Bluebeard's control. Each time he lies over the woman's body, the tape plays by itself, despite his efforts to turn it off. As it happens with many props used by Bausch onstage, the tape acquires multiple roles throughout the piece. It sometimes stands in the role of an outside narrator, observing and judging the characters. Other times, it seems to impersonate emotions, like those of curiosity, oppression or fear. In this scene, it represents the woman's disobedience provoked by curiosity and fear, which lead her to open the forbidden chamber in Perrault's story, or to insist that Bluebeard does it for her, as in Bartok's version. The "disobedience" is repeated over and over, expanding the interdiction and its violation, creating a spiral of frustrations.

The violence in which he continuously jumps over her and drags her across the floor suggests rape, to which the woman eventually offers no resistance. Here, rape substitutes for the assassination in the Perrault and Bartok plots. But the audience's desire for further narrative developments and continuity is broken by Bausch's incessant manipulation of contradictions. The woman's passivity to rape dissolves into affection as she eventually hugs him back. As Servos has pointed out, this kind of ambiguous interaction reveals the contradictory nature of emotions and social roles. The woman is the victim, but the uses this condition as a weapon. The man is the ruler and the victor, but, at the same time, he is the prisoner of his own self-image (54).

The piece evolves, focusing on this spectrum of contrasting emotions. Obsessive gestures and desperation work as emotional leitmotifs, expressed by gestures repeated to exhaustion. For example, the woman (Judith) starts running to the corners of the stage, collecting the leaves that covered the floor and placing them inside her skirt. Each times she does it, she slips her hands over her head, demonstrating her exhaustion. These multiple repetitions created a real sense of tiredness, presenting to the audience the obsessive violence of her act and simultaneously creating a singular perception of time and space.

Images of solitude, violence and exploitation acquire strength by Pina Bausch's manipulation of large crowds of performers. In this case, they work not as characters, but as resonances of emotional states, deriving from the essence of the Bluebeard-Judith relationship.

The forbidden chamber motif, with hidden piles of dead female bodies victimized by male oppression, is indicated by a line of women that enters the stage. Expanding her own victimization, Judith herself stands among the women, choosing different performers and presenting them for Bluebeard's approval. In doing so, she is turning each of them into sexual displays or objects of male dominance. One after another is exposed to Bluebeard, who nevertheless despises them all. The women stay in the same poses in which they were previously left for his approval, their heads down and their hair covering their heads in humiliation.

What seems to make a clear statement about men's domination over victimized women is followed by a twisted commentary. The other side of domination is displayed so as to show that women's subjugation can also be a form of domination. While the line of people moves onstage, the woman turns to Bluebeard who is now sitting on a chair. She sits on the floor next to him and caresses him with her hands, which nervously pass over his neck and face many times. This obsessively repetitive act becomes a threat: Bluebeard pushes her hands away, but they continue to reach for his face. A caress melts into an act of aggression. Or it simply reveals its opposite but intrinsic side.

In another scene, Bluebeard is seated on a chair. Many women lean their hands towards him and start shaking their long hair, tossing them over his face, spanking him with them. With subtle revenge, the women shift their status, from victim to predator.

The interweaving of emotional states is also translated through a generalized chaos. Twenty-five actors/dancers occupy the stage, the men continuously throwing their bodies against the walls, the women staring at them. One woman suddenly comes towards one of the man. While he is sus-pended in the air, she abruptly pushes him down by his feet, provoking him to fall, crashing his body on the floor. This act is furiously echoed by the other women who do the same with each of the men. Nevertheless, after the men are on the floor, the same women who had attacked them become compassion-ate and hug them, helping them to stand up again. The vio-lent and nonsensical tone of this scene is intensified by the noise of the bodies crashing against the walls, contrasting with the multiple, compassionate expressions that the women assume as the men fall down one by one.

Bausch's use of large crowds as a way to expand emotional states revisits the expressionists' search to transcend the indi-vidual scale and reach for universal emotional laws. But, dif-ferently from her predecessors, Bausch offers no real synthesis. Emotions keep splitting up in her pieces. On a structural level, the same denial of synthesis is present. There is no attempt to fuse into a total work of art, as defended by the Wagnerian ideal, endorsed by *ausdruckstanz* and the expressionists. Bausch does not share the German expres-sionist search of a true, essential art. While the monumentality of her work is often compared with that of Wagner, Bausch disagrees with his concept of the supreme art, synthesizing all artistic possibilities (*gesamtkunstwerk*).

Following the *Neue Sachlichkeit*'s frustration with reality, she does not believe it is possible to achieve wholeness. Her lan-guage of *tanztheater* may combine dance, opera, mime and spoken text, but these elements never blend. Like Brecht, she rejects synthesis, favoring a mode of representation that cuts across different media, each of which makes a different comment on the action/emotions. Chaos and dissonances substitute for theatrical harmony, and theatrical elements are exposed to their essentials.

In the course of the almost two-hour piece, the role of the protagonist shifts from Bluebeard to the woman/wife. In a peculiar scene, we hear loud laughs and noises from backstage, while the woman (Judith) turns around herself, in a whipping circular motion of the arms. Alone onstage, she becomes the center of the attention and temptation as a line of men gets close to her.

Surprisingly, instead of directly attacking her, these men start to show off their bodies in poses directed to the audiences, thus turning themselves into victims of a narcissistic impulse. One by one, they take off their shirts, then their pants, revealing multi-colored velvet briefs. They make poses, showing off their muscled bodies. But, eventually, their narcissistic display also works as a weapon of dominance. The woman moves in tormented circles around that menacing spectacle, until Bluebeard appears to "rescue" her. He hugs her close to his body in such a strong manner that it turns into suffocation. An act of protection dissolves into oppression.

Later, the piece depicts scenes where a large crowd wears white clothes and carries white pillows and bed sheets, elements that together work as symbols of sex, following the idea of marriage and honeymoon rituals that could relate to the story of Bluebeard and his recent wife. A group of dancers is onstage, the women in nightdresses, the men only wearing shirts. They all hold and shake bed sheets against the floor, continuously.

With one of the sheets, a man catches a woman who was dancing freely close to him. He folds his sheet around her body, wraps her with it, and carries her over his back, swinging her in the air, as if she were a bag. This action is echoed by the other men who, one after another, pile the women's bodies on a chair, one on the top of the other. As a response, the women start laughing nervously.

Loneliness is at the center of Bausch's view of the *Bluebeard* tale. It is a loneliness that applies to both women and men, since the former are oppressed as victims, and the latter have to struggle in order to maintain their strong images. This loneliness is abstractedly shown through gestures, and it is sometimes embodied through the use of props, as is the case of a plastic doll.

The stage is empty when a woman enters hugging an old, ugly, plastic and armless doll. She caresses the trashy doll as if it were a most beloved human being, places it on the floor and lies on the floor next to it and then leaves. Bluebeard, who was running around the stage in a *robe-de-chambre* suddenly sees the doll. The doll becomes a seducer, and his reaction is an insecure and narcissistic try to get its attention and approval. He takes off the robe, showing his bright yellow velvet brief, and starts making different poses to display his muscled body. Another woman in the corner stage laughs nervously at this scene and decides to compete with him for the doll's attention. Substituting for Bluebeard's muscles, she makeovers, covering her lips with red lipstick, and making sensuous faces.

At a certain point, the music significantly takes over the performers' actions, commanding them. Repeatedly, as the music plays, everyone is moving in scattering gestures and making noises. As the music stops, everyone suddenly stops too, echoing an action-response game played over and over again. It is as if overwhelming emotions such as curiosity and fear are governing their acts. The performers become chaotic marionettes.

Different layers of emotion are depicted through the presentation of layers and layers of clothes that the woman (wife) is obliged to wear. Near the end, couples dance in slow motion, their heads down, their bodies lying over one another. They start taking their clothes off, lying on the floor and rolling, their bodies coming close together. Bluebeard runs around them in nervous zigzags and begins taking their clothes from the floor. He, then, piles the clothes on the centerstage around the woman. Suddenly, he begins dressing her with a long-sleeved pink-grey dress, as she stays passive. He continues to overdress her, putting all the clothes around him on her, one on the top of the other until she leaves the stage, suffocated. At this time, the other performers are dancing alone, stretching their arms as if they were dancing with invisible partners, which could also be read as a reference of the phantoms of the dead wives. Then it becomes clear that Judith is to receive the same punishment as Bluebeard's previous wives.

At the climax of the operatic music, Bluebeard hugs the woman, hangs her and starts shaking her body, throwing it from one side to the other, as if she were a yo-yo. The other men repeat the same gesture with the other women, resonating Bluebeard's act of cruel manipulation. In the following scene, Bluebeard lies over the woman's body while she is totally passive. He pushes her body against his through the floor but she does not respond. She is already dead. He hugs her and claps as a way to wake her up, but she is deadly quiet. He then begins to clap desperately. His clapping suggests the obsessive acts of a child who acknowledges having done something wrong and therefore tries to undo it, playing as if it were only a joke. Each time his claps stimulate the other dancers to move and freeze, which in itself is turned into a children's game.

As it is repeated over and over again, the clapping also becomes a vignette that creates gestural patterns and organizes the action. Bluebeard claps while dragging his body and that of the woman which is glued to his, moving both closer to the edge of the stage as the stage lights darken progressively. This happens in a dissolving manner, each time with the performers responding to Bluebeard's clapping with poses that freeze and then change.

Bluebeard and the dead woman's body disappear in the middle of the other dancers' bodies. The dancers keep responding to the clapping, which each time resembles more the clicking of a photographic camera. They pose together smiling; then they dissolve in individual poses that tend to repeat and subsequently add up in gestural accumulations. The scene gets increasingly darker until the image fades out.

Bluebeard disappears. He is not killed by heroic and protective brothers. He actually kills the woman but he, too, dies quietly and insignificantly, like every common man.

Pina Bausch's *Bluebeard* is not about retelling a fairy tale. Bausch's piece is built from the emotions invoked by the idea of two human beings oppressing each other. In an hipper, realistic way, she makes use of exaggeration and repetition to uncover these emotions, exhaustively. Nevertheless, the insistence does not clarify the emotions. Nor does Bausch resolve them, positioning herself ideologically in relation to the issue. In contrast to literary fairy tales where violence is used as a moral lesson, with good inevitably winning over evil at the end, Bausch's violence is anarchic.

Throughout the piece, the spectator is confronted with violence, which is initially depicted through the relation between Bluebeard and his wife and later resonates through a large cast of performers involved in multiple, everchanging activities onstage. Through obsessive repetition, where each gesture can echo for more than ten minutes, Bausch suspends the notion of time, expanding it in a different, perhaps horizontal direction. Similarly, making use of a large, anonymous crowd that repeats the protagonists' movements and actions over and over again, she transcends the concept of individual characters, expanding their actions and turning them into the Everyhuman being.

Bausch reveals the fragmentation and lack of congruity of narrative to its extremes. In return, she continuously leaves gaps in the narrative in a way that obliges the audience literally to fill in these gaps. She substitutes a self-contained meaning for one that is only build up according to the previous references of the spectator.

Indeed, Pina Bausch denies being concerned with narrative when she is in the process of creating a piece (Bausch, personal interview, 1991). Together with her performers, she experiments with responses to emotional source material, which is translated into fragments of gestures, words or music. The repertory of gestures—touches, caresses, pushes, rubbing—is mostly common. What makes the gestures astonishing and sometimes shocking is the way they are combined and presented to the audience. For Bausch, meaning as a whole comes only *a posteriori* to the construction of scenes, and it is build in the forms of poetic articulations, according to rhythm, and cadence, and spatial design. Her work has a logic similar to that of poetry. As in written poetry, Bausch keeps the spectator active as (s)he has to open up different channels of perception to connect with diverse stimuli onstage. It is up to the spectator, bombarded by Bausch's performers with the insistence of time and repetition, to make his/her own connections within this fragmented universe of images. The lenght of Bluebeard, lasting 110 minutes, performed withouth intermission, forces the audience to participate in the dramaturgy, loading the piece with its own emotional responses (Servos 55).

As Nervos points out, if there is a logic in Bausch's work, it is that of the body and not that of the narrative, since the body escapes from the laws of casualty. Bausch's *tanztheater* deals with direct physical energy (22).

As a strategy to avoid narratization, Bausch provides with no character differentiation, since the performers constantly shift among *personae*, from quickly delineating a character to suddenly acting as themselves, for example. A differentiation between minor and leading roles is also non-existent. Bluebeard, although a "protagonist," becomes as anonymous as the other performers when the piece evolves, and his fate represents simply that of every man, every woman.

The scenic space is a blank, constantly being formed and renewed onstage as the performers come in and out of scenes. This constant vacancy is framed by the sets, made of live materials like earth, water and leaves and a few movable elements such as chairs. The costumes, dresses and suits, street shoes and high-heeled ones are typical men-and-women's clothes. They do not serve to impersonate, but they are questioned in their own function as outer skins of society's rules.

This sense of strangeness and the constant emotional shifts happen because of the way Bausch uses theatrical elements. Her work certainly aims for meaning, but it is a kind of meaning that subverts rather than resolves. Roland Barthes calls it the "third, or the obtuse meaning," which he calls the epitome of the counternarrative. It forms a tapestry of multilayering meanings which behave like a geological formation: it always lets the previous meaning continue, saying the opposite without giving up the contrary (*Image—Music—Text* 55-63).

And, echoing a common question among dance scholars and critics: is what Bausch does dance? In manipulating different artistic forms, she does not respect the traditional music-movement relationship. In reference to dance, the choreographer rejects the constant need for motion, whereas in theater, she rejects its literary references. Bausch is unceasingly questioning the codes and the rules of representation. Content and form are inseparable in her work. They amalgamate because they resist being analyzed separately.

With Bausch, the kinesthetic empathy and pleasure that we usually get from a dance performances is substituted by the empathy and pleasure for human variety, with performers with different morphological types, backgrounds, colors, languages. There is no seduction for virtuosity, with movements that the spectator cannot repeat. In Bausch's performances, the pleasure also comes with transgression or the orders of the spectacle, with the proximity of audience members with the diverse performers, who often seem to have deserted the representation to be simply themselves.

In fact, Bausch's creations are drawn from the personal creation of her devoted performers, grounded on their own reactions to emotional stimuli. Her motto is physiological, as she asks her dancers/actors to respond through performance to certain emotional stimuli, for example, memoriesr of birthdays, feelings of pain or love.

Pina Bausch does not provide for an analysis of the causes of oppression between men and women but rather deals in its mechanisms. She dissects them, presenting every possible form of oppression with a fatalistic vision. She sees people mechanically responding to stereotypical expectations, presenting behavioral schemata, longings, and cliched roles as existential conditions (Servos 55). Bausch shares with Maguy Marin the same interest in conventions and stereotypes, but their attitude towards them is harshly opposed. While Marin parodizes cliches, criticizing them in an expectation of change, Bausch is a fatalist, seeing the world as a *huis clos*. In her pieces, the impossibility of communication is sedimented through never-ending repetitions.

Bausch's fragmented style, coined from forms such as vaudeville, music hall and revue, translates a generalized dis-illusionment with historical references, with imposed narratives and images. What she does parallels literary deconstruction as she acknowledges the instability of language and communication and does not provide a harmonious, one-to-one set of correspondences between the levels of the signified or concepts in language (Derrida).

Pina Bausch deconstructs the emotional repertory of human beings, approaching her work to the psychoanalytical theories of Jacques Lacan. For Lacan there is no separation between the self and society because society inhabits each individual, from the moment (s)he dominates the social institution of language. This vision parallels Bausch's interweaving the political/social with the personal in her work.

Lacan's texts are constructed in an associative style that is not assertive. They are based on word games, symbols and signs that are intended to subvert the normalization that everyday language exposes. The same attitude is present in Pina Bausch's intention to subvert characterization and role playing in performance, as well as the way we interpret emotions.

The impossibility of communication, in Bausch, between men and women, is echoed in Lacan's idea that human beings are born with a sense of loss or a lack developed by their impossibility of being both sexes at the same time. The acknowledgment that the other sex is unattainable provokes a fatalist frustration (Benvenuto and Kennedy).

Emotions are central to Lacan, but he believes that they cannot be reached directly, because they are mediated by the imperfect means of language. According to him, there is no stable relation between the signifier and the signified and we do not often say what we feel or feel what we say. It is exactly this kind of disencounter and emotional friction that Pina Bausch aims to depict in her work. Approaching the fragmented and incongruent formations of the symbolic, the choreographer strives to outwit the rational and access the more authentic subtexts of the unconscious.

On another level of analysis, the emotional contradictions and the lack of continuity in the narrative presented by Bausch can also relate to the structure and meaning in the fairy tale. Folklore analyst Max Luthi explains that contradictions are always at the heart of every fairy tale. Situations and emotions exist only to generate their intrinsic opposites. A lack is created to generate a fulfillment and an interdiction is an invitation to violation (55)

In his psychoanalytical analysis of *Bluebeard*, Bettelheim sees it as a story of sexual temptation. He points out the gender ambiguity of the name Bluebeard, attesting that the name, which in French is La Barbe Bleu, could apply to both masculine and feminine (282).

Bausch's fragmentation of the narrative parallels the peculiar way in which *Bluebeard* was constructed. The story was probably invented by Charles Perrault based on motifs existing on Scandinavian and Russian folklore and perhaps in one of two Breton real-life cases. But the author certainly did not know exactly how to fill gaps in the tale, leaving it fragmented, with various inconsistencies in the plot. For example, there is a gap in the narrative, between the wife's entering the forbidden chamber and Bluebeard's unexpected return. Likewise, Bluebeard's willingness to wait a quarter of an hour before killing her kis somehow unconvincing (Opie and Opie 133).

Bausch does not retell fairy tales. Yet, despite her subversive approach to narrative, fairy tales as prototypical narrative are very important to Bausch. (Bausch, personal interview, 1991). Her interest is particularly focused on the fairy tale as "myth" or cultural artifact, because it provides the choreographer with important material about the dehumanizing effect of cliches and social conventions. This is the side of the fairy tale that the choreographer tried to explore while creating of the piece *Bandoneon*. The process was reported in Raimund Hoghe's book, who co-wrote the piece's text, following the company from October to December 1980, when it premiered. Important source materials for the creation of the piece's scenes were fairy tales, used there to stimulate the performers' memories and emotional repertory. The different phrases, germinated from the memory of the performers, coming from different countries and cultural backgrounds, remembering diverse tales. Nevertheless, despite the differences, they all related to similar cliches that homogenized and mythicized the stories, as they are known today through anonymous literary collections, Disney films or TV commercials worldwide:

> I'm Cinderella and the shoe fits me...Now the Emperor has a mechanic rouxinol but I'll wait until it agonizes and will chant for him...I'm Little Red Hiding Hood and I look forward for my wolf at gramma's ..I've already thrown 11 shoes against the wall but there were no prince's inside any..I'm Sleeping Beauty and I've been sleeping for 99 years. I hope something happens quickly! I'm Pinnochio and I start to live (130-131).

7

Kinematic's Reconstructed
Girl Without Hands

The New American Dance

In 1980, three dancers grouped together and began to experiment with choreography. Tamar Kotoske, Maria Lakis and Mary Richter called their group Kinematic, a term reminiscent of kinetic (bodies in motion) and cinematic (filmic devices). Although the group's name relates to pure movement terms, Kinematic's main interest with the medium evolved towards the creation of stories and the relationship between dance and verbal texts.

Maria Lakis, Mary Richter and Tamar Kotoske met in New York City in 1980, when they were working as dancers in the companies of Timothy Buckley, Bebe Miller and Nina Wiener, choreographers of the new generation of the New York city downtown performance scene. While these new dance groups were aesthetically concerned with narrative and certainly influenced Kinematic's appetite for meaning, the three women were still unsatisfied with the way the others were telling stories and looked for a discourse of their own.

Kinematic's members dance backgrounds are eclectic. Before dancing in New York, Tamar Kotoske received a B.F.A. in dance from Case Western Reserve University in Cleveland, Ohio, and danced there with Footpath Dance Company. Currently she is investing in her acting skills. Maria Lakis received her B.F.A. in dance from Ohio State University and worked with Thom Fogarty and Nina Wiener & Dancers. Recently, her main interest has been focused on clowning. While experimenting with postmodern choreography, both

Kotoske and Lakis studied ballet with Pamela Citelli. Mary Richter was a member of Nina Wiener & Dancers. Trained at the Dayton Ballet, North Carolina School of the Arts and Ohio State University, she became increasingly oriented towards the bodily mechanisms, studying physical therapy methods and techniques.

Kotoske, Lakis and Richter's artistic background shaped their interdisciplinary interest in dance, literature, mime and theater. Kinematic amalgamated language represents a new generation of artists who have been working alongside contemporaray trends in dance-theater, live installations, and performance art.

Since the group's beginnings, Kinematic's founders have created, directed, and performed their works. It was in 1983, after three years of collaboration on various dances that the women decided to use verbal texts. The piece *Unilateral Neglect* (1983) was a duet where Tamar Kotoske and Mary Richter moved over the sound of fragmented quotations, extracted from medical journals. The articles discussed aphasia, a neurological disease where the left part of the brain is deficient, causing language problems.

Another important step toward the performance style the group built up with the fairy tale dances came with the use of characters and storylines. An interesting example of how Kinematic's members see the concept of storylines is *Dark Ride*. Composed in 1985, the thematic source of this dance was a Victorian melodrama. In this dance, Kinematic explored different rooms of a Victorian house where many scenes occurred. Afterwards, in 1986 the three women became more literary, using texts from recognizable sources and devoting their work to storytelling through dance.

Kinematic's use of eclectic theatrical elements places its work alongside contemporary trends in dance, theater and performance art. The three women work on a collaborative basis, both creating and performing the works.

Kinematic's members has created a significant fairy tale dance trilogy. It consists of *The Snow Queen*, based on Hans Christian Andersen's story and presented in 1986 at Dance

Theater Workshop in New York; *The Handless Maiden,* based
on the Grimms' tale and shown in 1987 at The Home for Contemporary Theater; and finally *Broken Hill,* adapted from the
Grimms' *The Worn Out Dancing Shoes* and presented in 1988 at
Dance Theater Workshop.

The first idea for using fairy tales in dance arose from feelings of nostalgia. Mary Richter suggested to her colleagues the
use of Andersen's *The Snow Queen* because it had been her
favorite story as a child. The idea was immediately accepted by
the two others.

Fairy tales were perfectly suited to these women's artistic
concerns of building formalist interplays without neglecting
meaning. Fairy tales are recognizable texts, a part of everyone's childhood, and therefore they could be played with easily and still remain familiar to audiences. The poetry of fairy
tale stories—where animals, plants and humans are vividly
animated—represented rich material to be explored in theatrical terms. The way that actions lead to an end where good
always destroys evil responded to Kinematic's attraction to
archetypes and the collective unconscious; all are avid readers
of Carl Jung. At the same time, fairy tales have renewed the
women's fascination with childhood.

Above all, they consider fairy tales stories that allow anything to happen, where characters appear and disappear with
no need for a realistic development. Episodic and stylized,
fairy tales include elements of magic and present a fairly
transparent structure, allowing the group's shifts of character,
plot and point of view (Kotoske, Lakis, Richter, personal interview, 1988).

Kinematic used spoken text associated with movement to
delineate a unique type of narrative dance. The script "tells
the story" and, at the same time, becomes an additional source
for structural composition. Rather than being preoccupied by
clarifying a literary plot, the fairy tale dances explore the formal interactions between words and movement. The interplay
of words and gestures becomes a narrative itself, creating a
wide spectrum of emotional responses generated by the rever-
berations and resonances between the two media.

Literary Bodies, Words in Motion

Kinematic's use of spoken texts with movements onstage revisits a tradition in the history of dance. In the development of Western theatrical dance, content was mostly presented outside the dance medium. Within the universe of narrative-dance, a variety of devices have been used in order to imprint meaning on an essentially non-verbal medium, including librettos that pre-establish the plots, mimetic gestures, descriptive musical composition, and scenery and props that decode narrative conventions. One method of installing meaning in dance has been to appropriate language and language-like systems. In sixteenth-century France, Jean Antoine de Baif was probably the first to conceptualize the combination of dance with music and text. He founded an academy to attempt the revival of the chorus of Greek tragedy with its synthesis of theatrical elements, but his ideas were not put into practice. (Cohen, S.J., *Dance as a Theater Art* 8).

The amalgamation of dance and text was actually inaugurated by Balthasar de Beaujoyeulx. In his *Ballet Comique de la Reine* (1581) theatrical elements were employed to clarify the mythological battle between Jupiter and Circe. The dance combined recitation, movement and song, to serve as propaganda to illustrate the power and prestige of the French court. Nevertheless, Beaujoyeulx's formula was not carried on, and the use of spoken text in performances with a single dramatic action was not developed.

Afterwards, in the *ballet-a-entrées*, particularly developed by the master and choreographer Monsieur de Saint-Hubert in seventeenth-century France, independent but thematically related scenes were presented on the stage, concluding with a grand dance in which all the characters appeared together. Badges were used to identify the characters on stage, and librettos explained the story to the audiences.

In England, the masques evolved as a form of *ballet-de-cour* borrowing elements both from the Italian masquerade and the French *ballet-a-entrées*. It combined dialogue, song, music and dance and ended with 'revels,' where the dancers invited the audience to join them in the dancing (Cohen, S.J., *Dance as* a

Theater Art 9). In 1661, Moliere created a new theatrical form which again brought text and movement together. His first *comédie-ballet*, *Les Facheux*, used the *ballet-a-entrées* to fill the time when the actors changed costumes. For entertainment, dancing sections were incorporated into the spoken comedy. In time, the movement interludes increasingly became linked to the narrative.

With the codification of the balletic vocabulary and the appearance of professional dancers on stage in the beginning of the eighteenth century, spoken texts were abandoned. Ballet language acquired mimetic conventions and used pantomime to "speak" on its own. The British choreographer John Weaver, who created the ballet *Loves of Mars and Venus* in London (1717), considered dance as an art or science, imitative and demonstrative (Cohen, S.J., *Dance as a Theater Art* 52). This choreographer felt that in dance, narrative should be entirely understandable through the use of dance and mime.

Words or badges identifying plots were replaced by dancers who were acclaimed for their great expressiveness. Marie Salle, for example, became a celebrity after creating a sensation in London for her performance in *Pigmalion* (1734). In the romantic ballet era, the idea of gestural expressiveness was increased by technique innovation: *port de bras* and pointework expanded the ballerina's gestural vocabulary and her potential for expressivity. Afterwards, in the nineteenth century, the ballerina combined her technical skills with dramatic powers in order to impersonate ethereal beings and supernatural lovers (Cohen, S.J., *Dance as a Theater Art* 70).

American modern dance used spoken texts in few productions, such as in Martha Graham's *American Document* (1938) and *Letter to the World* (1940) and Doris Humphrey's *The Shakers* (1931) and *Lament for Ignacio Sanchez Méjias* (1949).

In American modern dance, the combination of text and movement served to reinforce the dramatic expressiveness and to identify the narrative. Whenever words and gestures were combined, they would always remain different media: the two channels would never blend or become elements for simple formalist interplays.

In Doris Humphrey's *The Shakers,* for example, two spoken lines translate expressive, yet not mimetic movement performed by a group of dancers. While everyone moves, one of the dancers repeats: "My life, my life, my carnal life! I will lay it down because it is depraved." Without this cry, it would have been difficult to understand the meaning of that ecstatic worship (Jowitt, *Time* 9).

Martha Graham's *Letter to the World,* based on the life and work of Emily Dickinson, uses a dual main character: One Who Dances and One Who Speaks. They occasionally perform mirroing movements, but always remain separate personae (Siegel, *Shapes* 177).

With the emergence of the postmodern dance of the Judson generation, however, words were re-examined and eventually used as a sound accompaniment. Instead of thinking of words as an additional theatrical element for the sake of the narrative, the Judsonites questioned the possibility of words being dance *per se.* Douglas Dunn embodies this idea in his poem *Talking Dancing*:

> Talking is talking
> Dancing is dancing
> Not talking is not talking
> Not dancing is not dancing
> Talking is talking & not talking
> Dancing is dancing & not dancing
> Not talking is not talking & not not talking
> Not dancing is not dancing & not not dancing
> Talking is not dancing
> Dancing is not talking
> Not talking is not not dancing
> Not dancing is not not talking
> Talking is dancing
> Dancing is talking
> Dancing is talking
> Talking is dancing
> Not dancing is not talking
> Not talking is not dancing
> Dancing is talking & not talking
> Talking is dancing & not dancing
> Not dancing is not talking & not not talking
> Not talking is not dancing & not not dancing
> Dancing is not dancing
> Talking is not talking

Not dancing is not not dancing
Not talking is not not talking
Not dancing is not dancing
Not talking is not talking
Dancing is dancing
Talking is talking (qtd. in Banes, *Terpsichore* 200-201).

Structuring this poem in the same way he and his colleagues structured their dances—through analytic, self-revealing mechanisms—Dunn parallels talking and dancing, stressing both concepts and concluding that they are separate elements. The Judson choreographers, however, understood that when hearing sounds and simultaneously seeing movement, an audience would tend to combine them, and the results of the amalgamation could be very striking. With this idea in mind, many Judsonites started experimenting with the analogies that words-plus-movement could offer.

In Trisha Brown's *Primary Accumulation with Talking Plus Water Motor* (1973), for example, the verbal text is a task to be accomplished together with movement. Brown performs gestural motifs that are gradually being added into a growing phrase, while she speaks. The resulting dance comments on the difficulty of performing accumulative gestures while telling a story. As spectators, we tend to accumulate both gestures and spoken text into a single narrative.

Although Kinematic's members have turned to fairy tale narratives during the late eighties, they were not simply rejecting analytical postmodern dance values. They incorporated devices from their predecessors in the way they combined their interest for storytelling with an intense questioning of the mechanics of narrative and the structural possibilities of the dance medium.

The group uses stories as a frame to play with structure. In their fairy tale dances, Kinematic makes it difficult for audiences to identify with the dancer's characters by adding meta-commentary to the stories and by interrupting the narrative with comments about their own lives and the art world. Kinematic's references to fairy tales are personal. The tales are translated into the choreographers' own context, tinted with a postmodern sensibility and punctuated by explicit meta-commentary passages.

Kinematic's fascination with popular entertainment and mass media—its fairy tale dances include the use of TV images, folk songs, rock-and-roll, boogies and Latin music—was influenced by the pop art sensibility of the sixties. The group revisited the idea of combining high and low culture, following the same devices introduced by earlier postmodern choreographers. For example, Twyla Tharp's *The Big Pieces* (1971) is a recollection of music in Fred Astaire movie references. The piece juxtaposes popular forms such as baton twirling and tap dancing with ballet, mixing Haydn and Bix Beiderbecke.

In fact, Kinematic and the new generation of American choreographers go beyond the use of popular songs and movement references in their choreography: they also use the music-plus-image dynamics' superimposition brought by the television videoclip age. In the videoclip, the editing techniques allow the scenes to be structured without a causational narrative. As audiences, we are used to the videoclip episodic narratives, where personae are exchanged. From scene to scene, the clip's star shifts from performer to the character of a story created in the background in order to intensify the song's emotional mood. The new dance applies the videoclip's fragmentation, using episodic narratives and shifting personae's ideas. Kinematic's dancers shift between representing the story's characters and remaining artists during meta-commentary sections of the pieces.

From Script to Performance

Kinematic's scripts are collages. The group takes the literary fairy tale texts and fragments them haphazardously. Here, they revisit a postmodern strategy inaugurated in the dance field by Merce Cunningham. In the late fifties, Cunningham and his partner John Cage decided to apply chance procedures to the creation of choreographies and music. Based on the Chinese book of change, the *I'Ching*, which can be con sulted with the throwing of coins, Cunningham and Cage invented choreographic chance procedures, where a series of gestures received different numbers and were then put together according to the throwing of coins and procedures alike.

Kinematic's choice for composing the fragmented texts was mainly that of "geometric chance"—they would cut pages of the fairy tale books in half and use only one side of the page, for example. Eventually, they would use other written sources that would also be fragmented and then juxtaposed with the fairy tale texts. Besides the reference in the dance world to Merce Cunningham, Kinematic's textual fragmentation procedures directly refers to Derrida's notion of deconstruction. It implies a method of reading a text that reveals its failure as a sign; the standards or definitions which the text sets up are used reflexively to unsettle and shatter the original distinctions. In cutting pieces of the original fairy tale text and reassembling them with other texts in a textual collage, Kinematic endorses Derrida's view of language as an unstable and temporal process. Meaning is not immediately presented in a sign and there is no set one-to-one combination between signifiers and signifieds, as they constantly break apart and reattach in new combinations (Sarup 34-37).

After the fragmented text is completed, the group embodies them in gestural terms. Movements are created in improvisational ways, according to the emotional response the dancers/choreographers had to the words. This does not mean that the movement is mimetic or denotative. Most of the time, the emotional responses came from the sound of the words and not from their grammatical content (Kotoske, telephone interview, 1989).

The words-and-movement relationships are worked out in new ways, in a procedure reminiscent of the Judson choreographers' earlier composition workshops, where choreographic material was created through the accomplishment of verbally dictated tasks.

The way Kinematic performers insist on continuously gesturing during the spoken text sections makes it appear that the movement makes sense for them. But since we cannot decipher that code, we have the impression that they are using the code of another culture, with different denotative rules.

At first, that sensation of strangeness makes the movement seem abstract. But after some time, words and movement start to mesh. Although the dance does not mimetically respond to the words, the performers establish a system of correspondences that, when successful, can often lead the audience towards an intuitive recognition.

Kinematic works use limited, contained movements. Gestures are repeated over and over. Through the use of repetition, the group appears to reveal a gesture's inner mechanism, as if it were being studied in an anatomy class. At the same time, the group makes use of action verbs within the scripts to describe metaphorically the characters' emotional states. For example, in *The Handless Maiden*, the agony of the King when he returns from a war to find that his wife and son have disappeared is translated as the narrator recounts his movements:

> The young King began to weep, shrieking and wailing for none to see and hear. He was dashed against the cliffs and smashed into the splitering midnight, spinning endlessly on the pointed corpse of darkness.

Parts of the body can become metonymic signs of emotions. In the story, when the narrator says: "They were hands," he is expressing the union of the King and the Queen. In the end of *The Handless Maiden*, the narrator summarizes: "...they danced to from where they came," equating the concept of dance with happiness or with the traditional fairy tale ending: "they lived happily ever after."

For Kinematic members, words and movement only make sense when perceived as a whole. Neither the fragmented scripts nor the movements are individually sufficient to make the stories clear. In Kinematic's dances, the verbal information is added to the visual information of movement, creating a third, new meaning through the cumulative effect of these synchronically presented stimuli.

Narrative Structures

The Girl Without Hands was published in the Grimms' collection, since its first publication in 1812. Although its origins are unknown it has been demonstrated that the motif of a girl's hands cut off by her father is consistently presented in Eastern European folklore, particularly in Romenia (Degh, *Studies in Eastern European Folk* 319-365). Alan Dundes tells that in the Romenian oral version, an emperor who was left a widower is unable to find a wife as beautiful as his daughter. He then decides to marry her. As the daughter tries to flee, he cuts off her hands from the wrists ("Psychoanalitic Study" 60).

An analysis of Kinematic's *The Handless Maiden* will follow a synchronic description of its narrative source, the Grimms' *The Girl Without Hands* story, according to Vladmir Propp's classification. According to folklore analysis, the fairy tale is AT n. 706. Propp's classification follows:

(a) A lack. There was a miller who was very poor. In order to become richer, he makes a deal with the Devil/Lucifer.

(μ^3) Coersion/deception. The devil tricks the miller. In exchange for making him richer, the Devil makes the miller promise "whatever stands behind his mill," which the man thought to be an old apple tree.

(λ) Preliminary misfortune. In panic, he realizes he had promised his own daughter to the Devil.

(δ') Order violated. Nevertheless, the day the Devil returns to get "what belonged to him" he is unsuccessful. The girl was very clean, washed her hands well, and drew circles around herself, so that the Devil/Lucifer could not get a hold on her.

(δ^2) Order carried on. The Devil, furious, demands the miller cut his daughter's hands off, so he can come back to pick her up. To save her father, the girl allows her father to do it.

(A⁶) Mutilation. The father cuts her hands off

(G) Transference to a forest. The girl then, instead of waiting for the Devil to come and take her, runs away towards a forest. After running for days, she gets close to a pear tree. Although she is very hungry, she only takes one pear to eat.

(D²) The hero is interrogated by the donor. A guard catches her eating the pear that belonged to a kingdom and brings her to the king, who interrogates her.

(K) Liquidation of initial misfortune. The king immediately falls in love with her.

(W) Wedding. He marries her and gives her silver hands.

According to Propp's classification, the Grimm's *The Girl Without Hands* is a double fairy tale. As Propp has shown, this is justified by the fact that the tale is composed of two moves (*Morphology* 93). This includes an initial cycle that begins with a lack, develops and has a wedding as a *denouement* and a new one, which begins with a departure and an act of villainy and ends with a positive result.

(↑) Departure. The King goes to a war and leaves his queen pregnant, under the auspices of his mother.

(A) Villainy. The Devil intercepts a letter that the queen had written to the King, telling him about their new baby.

(L) Claims of a false hero. The Devil rewrites the letter, telling the king that she had given birth to a monster. The king responds to his wife, saying that he is sad, but that they should bear the child anyway. The Devil intercepts his response, ordering the King's mother to kill his wife and child.

(B⁵) Mediation. The queen mother (the Dispatcher), has pity on her daughter-in-law and, not understanding her son's wish, sends the young queen with her son to a forest.

(F) Receipt of magical help. In the forest, the young queen meets an angel who helps her. The angel makes the queen's hands grow up again.

(G³) The hero is led to a designated place. The angel protects her and places her in a small house in the heart of the forest.

(P) Pursuit of the hero. After the king comes back and asks for his wife, the queen mother tells him she has killed them, according to his orders. As the king dismisses it and is desperate, the queen mother reveals him that she has sent both of them to the forest. The king, then, rides to the forest in a desperate search that lasts seven years.

(o) Unrecognized arrival. At the end of the seven years, the king finds the small house and looks through the door. He sees a woman with a baby that could be his wife and child. Nevertheless, she has grown hands and therefore, he thinks it could not be her.

(Q) Recognition of the hero. The king realizes it is his wife, and she tells him about the angel.

(+) Positive result. The couple is reunited.

In Kinematic's *The Handless Maiden,* the literary fairy tale text from the Grimms was cut up and interwoven with random fragments from Carl Jung's *Man and His Symbols.* The result of the juxtaposition became a source for experiments with movement. Although the audiences could still recognize the original characters and identify the imagery, the story's causality was broken in the fragmentation process. Thus, episodes substituted for chronology, creating an opportunity for ideas from others sources to intersect with the tale.

As a step by step procedure, the group listed paragraphs or simply phrases taken from the Grimms' *The Girl Without Hands* at random, as they opened and closed the pages of the book. Then, Kinematic haphazardly borrowed words, phrases or simply ideas from Jung's *Man and His Symbols*. For instance, the section that introduces the Devil suggests archetypal ideas:

> The old stranger echoed under his rotten breath, "My stories could open all the dead doors!" Then he laughed and with the hand of the executioner on his shoulder, he summoned the falcons from the west. All at once every box and chest grows darkness, closed with darkness and sudden wealth, human sacrifice and history.

In other sections, it is possible to actually identify words or phrases taken from the book. This can be seen, for example, in the section where the Devil comes to take the girl away from her father.

> The beautiful daughter was a very blank girl who had no model for three years of sin. When time therefore came for the evil fetch to hear her, fear made a God circle and cried, It washed her in a triangle from over the breast to the left, Pale and trembling, she fell into a passion dream of black and blood red. Placing her head where her feet had been, she wielded a stick of blue chalk and drew round her feet a circle of indigo powder and prayer. All night long she danced in spirals as the boots of Lucifer advanced.

The images of circles, passion dreams and Lucifer were specifically taken from *Man and His Symbols,* from the chapter called "The Archetype in Dream Symbolism" (67-99). There, Jung relates the case of a young girl who had a series of twelve dreams, which prophetically fortold her own death (Kotoske, Lakis, Richter, personal interview, 1988).

The choice of Jung's book was deliberate, since the group saw a connection between the tale of a girl without hands and Jung's psychoanalytical theory of the collective unconsciousness. Starting from Freud's concept of the "archaic remanants" — mental forms whose presence cannot be explained by anything in the individual's own life and which seem to be aboriginal, innate, and inherited shapes of the human mind — Jung came to the concept of "archetype" or "primordial image." The archetypes are inherited by our psyche, which carries patterns of the mind's development, since the most primitive stage of man's evolution. The archetype is a tendency to form representations of a collective motif — representations that can vary a great deal.

For Kinematic dancers, *The Handless Maiden* is full of archetypal imagery. The story relates "the cutting off of a woman's hands by a male authority, destroying her capacity to make things happen, her tools for achieving freedom. In the process of growing up and becoming a real woman, her hands grow again" (Richter, personal interview, 1988).

This interpretation is hinted at in Kinematic's version of the Devil's speech, in which he attests that he cannot take the girl away with him because of her clean hands:

> How could I get near those unwritten hands? They are quite furious and wept-on! They look almost like flowers, pretty and white. Yes, that is what they have been...and they have flown off their stalks and become real wings. I have always feared the night when she would see herself like other girls! Cut them off! Yes! And take the blue magic away from her!

As a disembodied voice starts speaking these phrases, Kotoske, Lakis and Richter are sitting on the floor. Slowly, Richter stands up and contracts her torso, as if she were defending her body against the menacing words.

Folklorist Alan Dundes attests to a general tendency of scholars to despise psychoanalytic analysis of fairy tales both because this type of analysis frequently ignores the different versions of the stories, simplistically focusing on a single version and thus generalizing a particular case, and because they claim that whatever is told in the stories translates the people's real experience. Nevertheless, although he agrees with the fact that most psychoanalytical analysis of the fairy tale is amateurish, Dundes claims that most fairy tales have indeed gone through symbolic transformations. In the case of *The Girl Without Hands*, he denies that the cutting off of a girl's hands by her father could reflect an actual custom ("Psychoanalytic Study" 58). He explains that this act is a symbolic transformation of the act of incest.

Just as in *Sleeping Beauty*, as the central motif of rape was considered taboo and was thus transformed by Perrault in the seventeenth century, *The Girl Without Hands* was symbolically recreated by the Grimms, according to their Christian values. And to demonstrate that the tale is indeed about incest, Dundes follows Propp's structural study that has led to a formula applicable to all Indo-European fairy tales. Propp's formula establishes that fairy tales begin with the dissolution of the initial nuclear family and the formation of a new one (62).

In the tale, the father wants to marry his own daughter. Dundes explains later that this is a case of projective inversion, whereas it is the daughter who really suffers from an Elecktra complex and wants to marry her own father. Thus, she is the one that gets punishment. The symbolism of the hand connects with the father having asked her hands in marriage and that is the symbol to be cut off (61).

These symbolic implications certainly influenced the Brothers Grimm in their reshaping of the tale. In *The Brothers Grimm*, Jack Zipes contrasts the different versions of this fairy tale, that from its 1812 publication to the last one in 1857 became each time longer, less direct and more Christian. The author relates the ramifications of the tale with the social conditions experienced in the context of the Grimms' lives, particularly that of Wilheim, the younger brother of the two and the one responsible for the changes in the later editions. As Zipes explains, the 1857 later version made the maiden more helpless, stoic, and dependent on the angel, a Christian figure nonexistent before this version. Zipes also relates the betrayal of the girl's father in the tale with Wilheim's father early death; the mistreatments that the girl suffers, he connects with Wilheim's having suffered from asthma and a weak heart and being himself mistreated in Kassel (124).

Lasting thirty-five minutes, *The Handless Maiden* is Kinematic's shortest piece. Although the Grimms' story of the same name is complex, encompassing many changes of scene and action, Kinematic decided to give the performance an austere scenic treatment. The gestural vocabulary is subtle and complex, set within a mosaic-like structure. Although the movement was choreographed after the script was set down, the gestures do not literally correspond to the words.

Movement sequences repeat and evolve, building up as the narration evolves. Kotoske, Lakis and Richter are the only performers. They each alternate taking all of the parts in the story—the Miller, the Girl/Queen, the King, the Queen

Mother and the Devil. The stage is bare. The set consists entirely of Stan Pressner's lighting design, which divides the scenes of the story with blackouts. There is no character differentiation through costuming: the three women wear identical dark tulle skirts over their leotards. The script is entirely narrated from off-stage by Jeffrey Logan and is punctuated by folk songs.

Kinematic divided the Grimms' story into three parts, respecting the traditional division consisting of introduction, development and conclusion. Thus, The *Handless Maiden,* is sectioned into "The Bargain," "Trials and Journeys" and "The Beginning." The ending section is significantly called a beginning, suggesting a never-ending state which is an idea that accords with all fairy tales, where the "once upon a time" and the "they were happily ever after" do not stand as real-time boundaries.

Although the movement is rarely mimetic, representing the spoken words, the dancers' gestures create a consistent emotional resonance to the simultaneous verbal narrative. This consistency is generated by a highly symmetrical structure created by the gestural composition in relation to the script. The formal organization replaces the need for complete sentences or visual information provided by set design and costuming. The symmetrical structure explains the development of the actions through repetition and small variations.

"The Bargain" section condenses fragments of the text, from the *(a)* to *(A^6)*. Here each woman moves separately to certain phrases spoken by the narrator and, at the end of the section, they move in unison. "Trials and Journeys" tells of the girl's adventures, from *(G)* to *(P)*. This section is composed of group movements and a more expansive use of space. "The Beginning," which tells of the encounter of king and queen in the forest, from *(o)* to *(+)*, is composed of three solos followed by a trio dance. This last section, which echoes the structure of the first, suggests a circle, a complete shape, which parallels the girl's regrowing hands and her search for wholeness.

The dance begins with the three women sitting on the floor as the narrator starts speaking. The movement, braided with spoken text, is alternated among the women. When the narrator talks about a poor miller, it is Mary Richter who gestures. When he speaks of the Devil coming towards him, Tamar Kotoske moves. When he presents the bargain dialogue between the Devil and the Miller, it is Maria Lakis who acts. Each woman individually moves to a sequence of phrases, and in the last section of phrases, the three dancers perform together, as if they were concluding a piece of action. "As all was finished and contrived, the Devil vanished." The narrator ends the section called "The Bargain."

At this time, the three women are seated on the floor. They move in place, yet their gestures have a harsh, scattered quality, which contrasts with their lack of mobility. This contrast creates a tense, frictional movement relationship, as if the women were imprisoned or asphyxiated in an emotional/physical situation.

After the three solos performed with abstract types of gestures, "The Bargain" evolves towards mimetically constructed gestural sequences, which translate the group's desire to build up more explicit statements about the Girl's suffering, her obedience towards the Father and the Devil's prototypical evilness. Here each of the three women performs a series of different gestures simultaneously, sometimes relating to each other in a motion dialogue. "Dear father, I am your devil, and you are mine. Cut my fingers where I begin and where I end...the hand is yours," the narrator says. Mary Richter, sitting on her knees, straightens her arms and gives her hands to Tamar Kotoske, who takes them but looks to the opposite side (as if she and the Father were ashamed of having to cut his daughter's hands).

At that moment, Maria Lakis, alone at the front stage, repeats gestures that bring her hands over her neck and face, covering herself. She mimes hands being cut off. At this moment, she seems to be a storyteller, translating to the audience in a direct way the shame and the terror of the situation. When the narrator says, "The Devil agreed it was splendid," Kotoske mimetically represents the Devil's part. She sticks her fingers over her forehead, simulating horns.

During "Trials and Journeys," the women travel in space in a flowing sequence of movements. They suddenly stop in freeze-poses, dissolve them and begin other movement sequences. These gestural patterns may be seen as a parallel to the story of the Girl's own journeys and escape to the forest from *(G)* to *(G³)*.

She goes from one place to another, escapes the Father, the Devil, and the King. In her misadventures, one situation dissolves into another. Her body is cut and fragmented.

In this section, folk songs from Turkey and New Guinea respectively are blended with the spoken text. During the music sections, the movement compositions echo the preceding gestures performed to words, a procedure that expands upon visual allusions. Bit by bit, new variations are added to the original movement, making it more elaborate. This gestural organization works as a metaphor for multiplying emotional states.

For instance, the narrator's voice says: "She stretched far over the moor and woman water, into mud and the frightful great moment. She went strange with touching red fancies in sad humor, and could not sense opinions for weeks." The three women are sitting on the floor, walking in circles, like dogs following their own tails. As they turn their heads down, a Turkish song begins to play. The performers turn their heads up, do their dog-walk again, turn their heads down, straighten their legs up and down, and turn their heads up again very slowly, one by one. The movement's repetition imparts a sense of the prolonging of the Girl's anguish.

The ending section of the dance, called "The Beginning," embodies the same parallel format as the dance's beginning. After the three women push their bodies against the stage wall, fall on the floor and stand up, they again sit on the floor. This return to a more constrained use of space relates to the intimacy of the situation, which involves only the king, the queen and their son.

As in the first scene, in *(o)* and, subsequently, *(Q)* each woman gestures to specific verbal sentences, one at a time. "Then he saw her living hands, which were not as simple as you may think ...," the narrator says. Mary Richter straights her hands and imitates waves with her torso, while the other two dancers are stationary. "There was no mistaking the free floating thumbs of the stars in the mounds of her pinkies ...," says the narrator, while Tamar Kotoske crosses her arms, straights her legs, and draws a vertical line in the space. Then Maria Lakis gestures. "But my wife had silver hands, said the King." She scratches the top of her head, mimes a bear and places her hand on her cheek.

In the end of "The Beginning," the three women are sitting on the floor with crossed legs. They pull their heads to the floor, straighten their legs and slowly roll up their bodies, until they are standing still. Then, they camber with their torsos backwards and start walking in circles. The pace quickens and the circles become larger. The performers run in space, jumping and leaping in circles. In centrifugal movements, they spread to the stage sides until they disappear.

That is how they present *(+)*. This is the first time that the women—representing the Woman/Girl/Queen altogether—claim the whole space and move freely in it, in contrast to the contained, broken and centripetal gestures of preceding sequences. The performers' shift in the movement quality responds to the story's development: at this time the Girl is a whole person again as she has regrown hands.

It is significant that movement here follows an internal organization that is structured by the alternations between gathering and scattering movements. In *The Handless Maiden*, the three women move in place, mostly while sitting on the floor. Yet, in opposition to the use of the space, their gestures have a scattering quality. In a nervous manner, the dancers repeatedly stretch their limbs to the extreme. Here, the space seems to be at once oppressive and frightening.

The suffocating and intimidating quality of space is reinforced by the fact that the performers do not communicate. There is no eye contact, even when the dancers move together. This quality of movement and posture gets replaced in the end—as well as in the folk song sequences that represent freedom—with scattering movements that occupy the full space. In these contrasting scenes, the performers open their bodies and eyes to each other.

The treatment that Kinematic gives to *The Girl Without Hands* corresponds to the logics of postmodern narration. Trachtenberg suggests that in the postmodern narration, the fast changes in content and context demonstrate that the meaning of language can no longer be controlled (14). This interplay between the world of perceptual narration and the world pre-narration creates narratives that are still anti-illusionist. In dance, what Kinematic has done is to present movement that is only partially expressive *per se*, but that acquires meaning when scrambled with words.

Allegory and Anti-Illusionism

In the book *Art After Modernism: Rethinking Representation*, Craig Owens includes a chapter called "The Allegorical Impulse: Toward a Theory of Postmodernism." His definition of allegory illuminates Kinematic's device of re-writing fairy tales, using these tales as cultural artifices.

Craig Owens defines allegory as an attitude as well as a technique, a perception as well as a procedure, occurring whenever one text is doubled by another. In the allegorical structure, one text is read *through* another, however fragmentary, intermittent, or chaotic their relationship may be (204).

In its wish to work with recognizable stories, Kinematic entered the realm of allegory. Jean Baudrillard claims that a derived representation corresponds better to contemporary reality than does invention. "Today no action, no feeling, no thought we own has not been performed by a thousand movies, commercials, television sitcoms, or magazine articles" (Wallis xvii).

Allegory is a device constantly linked with the postmodern sensibility, operating within the fragmentation of texts and the subversion of its pre-existing codes. Making use of allegory, postmodern art frees itself from the modernist myth of the originality of the avant-garde (Kraus) and the obsessive tradition of the slogan "make it new" (Rosenberg). Allegorical art manipulates fragments of discourses in a way that challenges their previous, authoritative claim to meaning (Ownes 205). The allegorical attitude also implies an overlapping of different artistic boundaries, proposing reprocity between the visual and the verbal. Visual works becoem texts, writing becomes a hierogliph (Owens 208-209).

In Kinematic's dances, fragmented scripts are interwoven with movement in unstable relationships, where meaning shifts between visual and auditory stimuli. These dances are allegorical, according to Owens's definitions, because, here, the fairy tales are read *through* other texts, which contain social and personal commentary.

In *The Handless Maiden,* the celebration of the marriage of the King with the Queen/Girl is described in the following phrase: "The King exchanged shoes with the bride, for that is more fashionable than YOU KNOW WHAT." The phrase works as an allegorical commentary on our society's honeymoon rituals.

Tourism as well as traditional anthropology are also satirized by the group. The fascination with exotic cultures in the postmodern era has been exemplified by the work of pop artists like Paul Simon, Peter Gabriel, David Byrne and others who explore sounds from Africa, the Caribbean and South America. Tourists travel to different countries and the mass media broadcasts large amounts of information on other cultures. The use of folk music works in *The Handless Maiden* as a counter-theme to the story. It breaks the continuity of the dance tale and, at the same time, illustrates a fascination with exoticism.

In the introduction to *The Post Modern Moment,* Trachtenberg talks about the anti-illusionist forces of allegorical art. As today texts emerge from the tradition of other texts, art becomes self-critic, reminding the reader/viewer of life rather than creating illusions (14-16).

In Kinematic's work, the fairy tale plots become collages of multiple discourses, retaining only a synoptic reference to the original tale. The combination of motion and speech in Kinematic's dances operates cinematically, without following chronological sequences.

The anti-illusionist impulse also appears in the way the group deals with personae. Story characters are shifted, frustrating the audience's wish for narrative. For instance, in *The Handless Maiden*, Mary Richter first offers her hands to her father to cut off. Just as the audience begins to identify her as the Girl Without Hands, Tamar Kotoske takes over the girl's part.

Anti-illusionist devices are used whenever the group wishes to break the audience's attempt to identify with the stories. Kinematic often announces that "this is a performance and not reality," by including scenes of metalinguistic discourse. By presenting its members as artists and performers, and by commenting on art and society, Kinematic transforms art into self-criticism. "This is not one story, that of the fairy tales. This can be many stories, including our stories as dancers..." (Lakis, personal interview, 1988).

Craig Owens points out that "the allegorical work tends to prescribe the direction of its own commentary" (204). In Kinematic's pieces, the tales serve as sub-texts to other commentaries. The storyline is often interrupted and punctuated by meta-commentaries, which allow Kinematic performers to jump out of the narrative and comment on their own situation as struggling new artists, on their works and on society. They criticize cliches, traditional gender roles and conventional behavior.

This can be seen, for example, in a scene of *The Handless Maiden* that describes the marriage of the King and the Girl/Queen. While Mary Richter twists her waist, rolls and tumbles, the narrator says "The King was bounding in his red striped marled-pasters, and the Queen displayed her astounding sideways balance." At that point, Maria Lakis and Tamar Kotoske express an appreciative "HUumm...," and applaud her performance. They recognize the beauty and playfulness of Richter's movement. In doing that, the women suddenly shift from performers to observers, reminding the audience that "this is a show, not real life."

8

Conclusion

Happy Endings in a Lost Paradise

Maguy Marin, Pina Bausch and Kinematic have created new, anti-mythical versions of fairy tales as their interpretations historicize the stories, placing them into context, revealing cultural, socio-political values shaped within the choreographers' working universe. By reopening the "classical" fairy tales for discussion in terms of their contexts and values, the three contemporary productions are questioning the *Cinderella*, *Bluebeard* and *The Girl Without Hands* stories in their institutionalized or mythic versions.

Historically, as Jack Zipes has explained, there had been great semantic shifts in the fairy tale through its literary adaptation of the oral folk tale of magic. These shifts were eventually suppressed, particularly since the advent of the publishing industry in the seventeenth century. Since then, the literary upper-class Western European versions of fairy tales have been spread in anonymous collections as *the* only tales there are.

The institutionalization that began in the seventeenth century has established a canon of tales, continually reproduced in each new fairy tale collection, film or advertisement. This canon is used to educate children and emphasize male adventure and power and female domesticity and passivity. It is used to legitimate white male European supremacy, as the dominant classes continue to shape the world in their own image (West, lecture, 1992)).

Innovative reinterpretations of the fairy tales solely can question the fact that fairy tales have a past and, hopefully, a distinctive future. They can point to the fact that the institu-

tionalized discourse of fairy tales, with docile princesses waiting for Prince Charmings to rescue them, are not the single
type of narrative representative of human storytelling tradition.

Only innovative reinterpretation of tales are able to comment on the semantic shifts occured over the process of writing the tales, pointing to the particular contextual characteristics of the stories. Only versions of the tales that are non-classi-
cal can become anti-mythical. And that is what Marin, Bausch
and Kinematic propose with their revisions.

De-Institutionalizing Artistic Categories

The same institutionalization vis-a-vis fairy tale stories happened in the dance medium. In that case, fairy tale dance productions have been repeating over and over again the exemplary Petipaean notion of the ever light and perfect ballerina
impersonating sweet heroines or smiling fairies. Petipa introduced ballet to the audiences in a way that parallels who we as
audiences continue to see it today: an art of symmetry, balance
and luxury, with ocasional storylines that are created as a gracious excuse for virtuosic display.

In contrast, the three fairy tale dance-theater productions by
Marin, Bausch and Kinematic are essentially anti-mythical, as
they use the postmodern strategy of appropriation in a way
that recuperates the contextual aspects of the fairy tale, earlier
frozen and invalidated through the mythicization process. In
"Myth Today," Barthes says that a myth is an appropriated
sign. For him, "myth" is speech stolen and restored, made with
specific signs of contradictory social discourses, transformed
into one normal, neutral narrative which "speaks us". The
author further attests that the best weapon against mythicization is to mythicize the thing in its turn, or appropriate the
very myth again (*Image — Music — Text*). In the case of fairy
tales, this means overtly presenting the stories as cultural
artifacts, which is exactly what the three contemporary
choreographers do in order to comment on them.

American critical theorist Hal Foster explains that this
"myth-robbery" process proposed by Barthes seeks in art to

restore the original sign for its social context. It resists mythification through a system of parodic collages. "In this bricolage, the false nature of these stereotypes is exposed as is the arbitrary character of the social/sexual lines that they define" (168). Marin, Bausch and Kinematic use these strategies to recreate fairy tale performatic narratives. Although, as artists, they do not deliberately follow specific philosophical or critical trends, these choreographers reflect theories and concepts embodied in their own historical context.

Marin incorporates postmodernism's fascination with convention and a cynical way of dealing with it. She uses the balletic code and depicts the dancers as mechanized dolls or automatons, parodying this universe of conventions and transcending it with good-humored but fierce social criticism. Pina Bausch and Kinematic work within the self-referential repertory of post-structuralist fragentation, a universe where the signified is denoted and the signifier made dominant.

This assertion responds to Ferdinand de Sassure's earlier structuralist theory of linguistics (1974). Sassure emphasized the distinction between the signifier and the signified. The sound-image of the word "table," for example, is the signifier, and the concept of a table is the signifed. A linguistic sign is derived of the structural relationship between the signifier and the signified and language is made up of these signs. Using Sassure's model, Kinematic's language is only made by signifiers, as neither words nor gestures are complete or form a concept in themselves. Nevertheless, when layered, they constitute a new linguistic sign, acquiring meaning.

In poststructuralism, there is no belief in one-to-one correspondences between propositions and reality. This view adopts different theories, according to the thinkers and philosophers that subscribe to it. Lacan, for example, wrote of the incessant sliding of the signified under the signifier. While strucutralism sees the truth as being "behind" or "within" a text, poststructuralism stresses the interaction of reader and text as a productivity—"reading has lost its status as a passive consumption of a product to become a performance" (Sarup 3-4).

These emphasis on interaction of reader and writer, and the preponderance of performance over text directly relates to Roland Barthes's confrontation between Work and Text (*Image — Music — Text*). Using Barthes's concept, it is possible to see the work by Marin, Bausch and Kinematic as Texts rather than Works, because they are open in themselves.

Barthes confronts the two terms in relation to the interdisciplinarity of much works being presented today. In contrast to Works, Texts do not fit into previous categories. As Barthes puts it, the interdisciplinary process that characterize Texts begins effectively "when the solidarity of the old disciplines breaks down." According to him, it is the difficulty in classification that becomes the point from which it is possible to diagnose a certain mutation in the fields of expression — a kind of relativization compared to what Einstein observed in science (156).

The choreographers' works demythicize the very concept of dance as they work in-between modes of classification. Marin who has been long known as a contemporary dance-theater *auteur*, has appropriated ballet and subtly reworked this style. Bausch frames her *tanztheater* within narrative themes but subverts any expectancy with narrative or character, using performers that shift between characters and universal types and a theatrical style that fragments movements, speech, music. Kinematic interweaves collages of gestures and words and juxtaposes them in unique ways. The choreographers clearly state that dance is not about travelling in space, performing jumps, turns or arabesques. Barthes explains that if the Text poses problems of classification this is because it involves an experience with limits. Marin, Bausch and Kinematic experience with the limits of storytelling in performance, using the most well-known cultural artifacts of our society to discuss and subvert social, cultural and moral notions implied in the institutionalized versions of fairy tales (*Image — Music — Text* 156).

As it happened with the resurgence of the Italian stage in the eighteenth century, transforming the notion and style of performance — at that time, dance was executed in low steps focusing on group patterns and, afterwards, became increasingly focused on virtuosic individual steps with legs pointed upwards in en dehors—dance has changed. As these three productions show, dance now substitutes the emphasis on travelling in space for gestural repetitions, performed in a way that connect the dance medium with mime and words. The works of Marin, Bausch and Kinematic question the need of new forms of expression or new artistic categories that include and acknowledge the developments of new media such as performance art, storytelling, or live installations. They confront the confortable use of preexistent artistic categories such as dance, or theater the same way that they confront our storytelling heritage. As Cornel West has said, the reproduction of old categories are symptomatic of our bureocratic mentality. They are less interested in tuning us with a better understanding of the world and of artistic mentality than they are focused on our accommodating with the discourses of power (lecture, 1992).

The postmodern, deconstructive universe where Bauch and Kinematic work is inhabited by third meanings (Barthes) and anti-illusionism (Owens). Within their contemporary fairy tale works, characters exchange within the performance and, using metalanguage to comment on our societal rituals, occasionaly become simply performers, the real people behind the masks.

In redesigning the approach to fairy tales, addressing them not only according to contemporary values but accessing intellectual theories that relate to the current contextual reality, these three artists demythicize fairy tales. They rewrite history using these prototypical narratives as tools to repaint, reaccess and subvert old, frozen texts.

Marin, Bausch and Kinematic reinvent fairy tales both in the way they present them and in the way they subvert lessons of *moralité* created by Charles Perrault in the seventeenth century. The ideology shaped by Perrault has continued to echo through our times, inhabiting household collections, Walt Disney films and a handful of commercials that use the examples of a patient sleeping beauty or a cleaning lady, namely Cinderella, with upper class dreams of luxury.

To these values, Maguy Marin responds with a commentary that is anti-bourgeois, as it ridicules and infantilizes luxury and thus diminishes its significance. Pina Bausch destroys Manichean notions contrasting men/women, dominator/victim. Her Bluebeard is not an evil man who kills poor, inoffensive women. For her, victims are dominators and human beings are not free to play single, voluntary social roles in life. Kinematic presents a girl/woman in the process of maturation, depicted through the symbol of regrowing hands, something that happens independently of the presence of a man. They see and state a women's process of wholeness as matter of personal growth.

Particularly since the dissemination of the printing industry in the seventeenth century, fairy tales have been presented to audiences as timeless, universal, and ageless stories. They are not and each rewriting has to emanate from the authors' or artists' own origins and context. Fredric Jameson claims the dangers of the incorporation of history as a text, since textualization shapes history's narrativization in the political unconsciousness. Considering that every text is social, historical and ultimately political, Jameson denounces allegorical interpretations that draw from the paradigm of other narratives without making their contextual changes clear. He highlights the importance of reasserting the the political content of individual fantasy-experience (*Political Unconscious* 22).

In rewriting fairy tales, Marin, Bausch and Kinematic have created new approaches to the writing and presentation of the tales. And their works represent only a few specific examples of the many new approaches that these stories can assume.

In contrast to the frozen version of fairy tales reproduced ever since they were written by Perrault in the seventeenth century and later by the Grimms in the nineteenth century, contemporary artists offer new anti-mythical versions of the stories. Parallel to the works by Marin, Bausch and Kinematic, contemporary writers offer new and anti-mythical interpretations of classical fairy tales (Carter; Sexton; Lee; Zipes). In "Transformations," for example, Anne Sexton questions the awakening of Sleeping Beauty, warning about women's "ressurected" lives as unbearable prisons dominated by male discourse:

I must not sleep
for while asleep I'm ninety
and think I'm dying.
Death rattles in my throat
like a marble (102).

And writer Judith Viorst changes the end of the Cinderella story with the lines:

I really didn't notice that he had a funny nose.
And he certainly looked better all dressed up in fancy clothes.
He is not certainly as attractive as he seemed the other night.
So I think I'll just pretend that this glass slipper feels too tight (qtd. in Zipes, ed., *Don't Bet on the Prince* 73).

The transformation of fairy tales over the years should accompany human beings' own storytelling tradition and development, as well as the evolution of civilization itself. Indeed, fairy tales demand continuous changes, according to sociohistorical contexts. These changes are dealt with by particular authors, in particular ways that should always be acknowledged. By clearly stating where they come from and where they are moving toward is ultimately the only way to rescue the fairy tales' utopian, magical — and why not? — educational potentials.

This need for constant revision of our storytelling repertory parallels Cornel West's concept of "fluidity." These revisions substitute pre-existent categories for an open, fluid and inclusive dialogue with the present reality in its different perspectives, ultimately unraveling the myths that have institutionalized and limited our discourses as human beigns (lecture, 1992).

Now, when the human race faces the end of a century, devastated by new wars, a generalized economical doom and the AIDS crisis, storytelling seems to reappear as an anchor for humanity's self-preservation and legitimization. Thus, instead of creating abstract works, artists are increasingly telling stories (Owens; Trachtenberg; Banes; Jencks). The art field witnesses a comeback of narrative and figurativism, and nightclubs and cabarets are filled with poetry-reading and storytelling performance art, while folk traditions are being revalued, together with the notion of multiculturalism in many academic fields. Paralleling *la mode des contes de fées* in the seventeenth century, we now face an undeniable fairy tale craze. Hopefully, at the present time, when academia has awakened itself to issues of multiculturalism and interdisciplinarity to confront the institutionalization of discourse, fairy tales will be increasingly re-examined and recreated in ways that are more representative of our heterogeneous and hybrid world.

Illustrations

1. Maguy Marin's *Cinderella*. (c) 1987 Graciela Magnoni, São Paulo, Brazil.

2. Bausch's *Bluebeard* for the Tanztheater Wupertal. (c) Gert Weigelt.

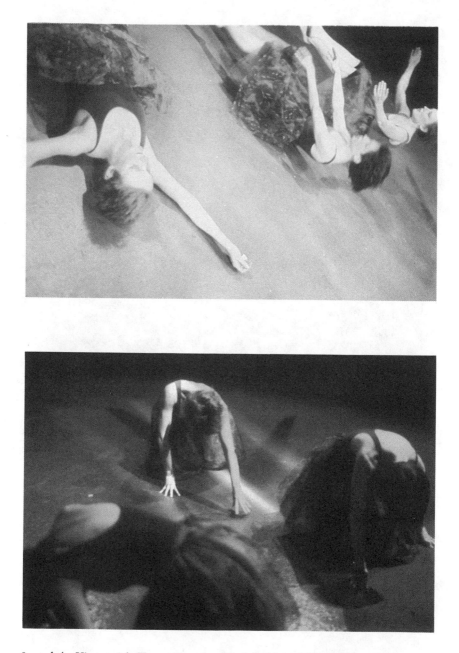

3. and 4. Kinematic's Tamar Kotoske, Maria Lakis and Mary Richter performing their *Handless Maiden* (c) 1987 Maria Lakis. Photograph by Julie Derscheid. Lighting design by Stan Pressner.

Bibliography

Dance

Adolphe, Jean-Marc. "New Dance in France." *Ballet International* 11 (1988): 22-26.

——. "The French Dance Scene – No Pause For Breath." *Ballet International* 12 (1989): 28.

——. "France/Dance of the 80s – What at Stake in a New Art?" *Ballet International* 13 (1990): 69-72, 182.

Aloff, Mindy. "Two Approaches To Dance." *The Next Wave Festival*, Brooklyn Academy of Music souvenir book (1987).

Anderson, Jack. "The Modern Dance." *The Dance Anthology*. Ed. Cobbett Steinberg. New York and Scarborough, Ontario: NAL, 1980. 418-431.

Aschengreen, Erik. "The Beautiful Dancer: Facets of the Romantic Ballet." *Dance Perspectives* n 58 Summer 1974.

Au, Susan. *Ballet & Modern Dance*. London: Thames and Hudson, 1988.

Balanchine, George and Francis Mason. *101 Stories of the Great Ballets*. New York: Dolphin, 1975.

Banes, Sally. *Terpsichore in Sneakers: Post-Modern Dance*. Middletown, CT: Wesleyan UP, 1987.

——. "Happily Ever After? – The Postmodern Fairy Tale and the New Dance." *New Dance: Questions and Challenges*. Montreal: Parachute, 1987.

———. "New Dance New York: the Eighties." Souvenir Program *Festival International de la Nouvelle Danse*. Montreal: Universite du Quebec, 1987. 52-65.

Baril, Jacques. *La Danse Moderne d'Isadora Duncan a Twyla Tharp*. Paris: Vigot, 1984.

———. "Kurt Jooss." *Les Saisons de La Danse*. Nov. 1975: 12-16 Beaumont, Cyril W. *Complete Book of Ballets*. Garden City: Garden City, 1949.

Béjart, Maurice. *Béjart by Béjart*. Trans by Richard Miller. New York: Congdon & Lattes, 1979.

Benson, Melissa and Susan Allene Manning. "Interrupted Continuities—Modern Dance in Germany." *TDR* 110 (Summer 1986): 30-45.

Bentivoglio, Leonetta. "Dance of the Present/Art of the Future." *Ballet International* 2 (1985): 25-28.

Beydon, Martine. *Pina Baush—Analyse d'Un Univers Géstuel*. Paris: Institut d'Études Thêatrales, Université de Paris III, 1988.

Birringer, Johannes. "Pina Bausch—Dancing Across Borders." *TDR* 110 (Summer 1986): 85-97.

Bonis, Bernardette. "Dance France Tanz." *Ballet International* 4 (1988): 18-22.

Canton, Katia. "Pina Bausch, Para Amar ou Odiar." *Jornal da Tarde* São Paulo, 7 June 1988.

———. "Vocâbulos Expressionistas." *Guia das Artes* São Paulo, n. 17 (1989): 40-43.

———. "Maguy, A Radical de Sapatilhas." *Jornal da Tarde*. São Paulo, 19 October 1990.

Carr, C. "The Essence of Dance." *Ruhr Works Journal*. New York: Goethe House (1989): 25-29.

Caroll, Noel. "The Return of the Repressed—The Reemergence of Expression in Contemporary American Dance." *Dance Theater Journal* 2 (Jan. 1984): 17-18.

du Chaxel, Francoise. "Maguy Marin: Une Danse des Depits." *La Danse, Naissance d'Un Mouvement de Pensee.* Val-de-Marne: Armand Collins, 1989. 163.

Clarke, Mary and Clement Crisp. *The History of Dance.* New York: Crown, 1980.

Cohen, Marshall and Roger Copeland. *What is Dance?* Oxford, New York, Toronto, Melbourne: Oxford UP, 1983.

Cohen, Selma Jeanne. "Dance as an Art of Imitation." *What is Dance?* Eds. Roger Copeland and Marshall Cohen. Oxford: Oxford UP, 1983. 15-22.

——, ed. *Dance as a Theater Art.* New York: Harper, 1974.

Cohen-Stratyner, Barbara Naomi. *Bibliographical Dictionary of Dance.* New York: Macmillan, 1979.

Copeland, Roger. "The Objective Temperament—Postmodern Dance and the Rediscovery of Ballet." *Dance Theater Journal* 4 (Autumn 1986): 611.

Coquelle, Jean. "The State of the Modern Dance in France." Trans. by Selma Jeanne Cohen. *Dance Observer* Dec. 1955: 145.

Cottias, Jacques. "La Venue de la modern dance americaine en France (1960-1970)." *La Recherche en Danse* n 3 (1984): 55-69.

Crisp, Clement and Edward Thorpe. "Contemporary Ballet". *The Dance Anthology.* Ed. Cobbett Steinberg. New York and Scarborough, Ontario: NAL, 1980. 397-418.

Daly, Ann, ed. interview "Tanztheater—The Thrill of the Lynch Mob or the Rage of a Woman?" *TDR* 110 (Summer 1986): 46—56.

——. "Classical Ballet: A Discourse of Difference." *Women and Performance* 3 (Spring 1987): 57-66.

——. "The Balanchine Woman: Of Hummingbirds and Channel Swimmers." *TDR* 131 (Spring 1981): 8-21.

Delahaye, Guy (photographs). *Pina Bausch*. Text by Raphael de Gubernatis and Leonetta Bentivoglio. Malakoff, France: Solin, 1986.

——. and G. Amsellem. *Cendrillon—Maguy Marin/Prokofiev*. Paris: Papiers, 1986.

Foster, Susan Leigh. *Reading Dancing: Bodies and Subjects in Contemporary American Dance*. Berkeley, Los Angeles, London: U of California P, 1986.

Fraleigh, Sondra Horton. *Dance and The Lived Body—A Descriptive*. Pittsburgh: U of Pittsburgh P, 1987.

Friedamn, Lise. "Kinematic's Choreography is Crazy Like a Fox." *Vogue* March 1987.

Garafola, Lynn. "The Travesty Dancer in Nineteenth Century Ballet." *Dance Research Journal* (Fall 1985/Spring 1986): 35:40.

Goldberg, Roselee. "Dance Theater." *Performance Art—From Futurism to the Present*. New York: Harry N. Abrams, 1988. 202-207.

Guest, Ivor. *The Dancer's Heritage: A Short History of Ballet*. London: The Dancing Times, 1979.

——. "The Age of Petipa." *The Dance Anthology*. Ed. Cobbert Steinberg, NAL, 1980. 374-382.

Hardy, Camille. "Myth Maker" in *Ballet News* (Spring 1986): 11-16.

Hoghes, Raimund. *Bandoneon—Em Que O Tango Pode Ser Bom Para Tudo?* Trans. Robson Ribeiro and Gaby Kirsch. Sao Paulo: Attar, 1989.

Jowitt, Deborah. "The Return of Drama: New Developments in American Dance" *Dance Theater Journal* 2 (1984): 28-31.

——. "Kinematic at DTW." *The Village Voice*. 28 October 1986.

——. "Telling Tales." *The Village Voice*. 14 July 1987.

——. "Talk to Me." *The Village Voice*. 14 July 1987.

——. *Time and the Dancing Image*. New York: William Morrow, 1988.

——. "Postmodern Dance." Seminar. Department of Performance Studies, Tisch School of the Arts, New York University, Spring 1988.

Kirstein, Lincoln. *Four Centuries of Ballet*. New York: Dover, 1984.

——. *A Short Historical of Classic Theatrical Dancing*. Princeton, NJ: Princeton, 1987.

Kisselgoff, Anna. "What Repetition is Doing to Choreography." *The New York Times* 19 October 1986: H7.

——. "The Dance: 'Cinderella' From Lyons" in *The New York Times* 22 January 1987.

——. "Dancing that Is Dazzling Distinctive." *The New York Times* 11 April 1988: H26.

Koegler, Horst and Joseph Lewitan. "In the Shadow of the Swastika." *Dance Perspectives* 57 (1974).

Kreemer, Connie. *Further Steps — Fifteen Choreographers on Modern Dance*. New York: Harper & Row, 1987.

Langer, Roland. "Compulsion and Restraint, Love and Angst: The Post-War German Expressionism of Pina Bausch and Her Wuppertal Dance Theater." Trans. by Richard Sikes. *Dance Magazine*. June 1984: 46-48.

Lesschaeve, Jacqueline. *Merce Cunningham — The Dancer and the Dance*. New York and London: Marion Boyars, 1985.

Louppe, Laurence. "The Origins and Development of Contemporary Dance in France." *Dance Theater Journal*. 7 (Summer 1989): 2-9

——. "French Dance: The New Narrative." *Dance Theater Journal*. 7 (Summer 1989): 34-36.

Manning, Susan Allene. "An American Perspective on Tanztheatre." *TDR* 110 (Summer 1986): 57-79.

——. and Melissa Benson. "Interrupted Continuities: Modern Dance in Germany." *TDR* 110 (Summer 1986): 30-45.

——. *Body Politic: The Dances of Mary Wigman*. Diss. Columbia University, 1987.

Mannoni, Gérard. Press Dossier of Maguy Marin. Paris, 1989.

——. "Cendrillon Au Ballet de Lyon — Une Autre Façon de Conter." *Quotidien de Paris*. 4 Dec. 1985.

Markard, Anna and Hermann. *Jooss*. Koln: Ballet-Buhnen-Verlag, 1985.

Michel, Marcelle. "Ballets-Féeries." *Le Monde*. December 5, 1985.

——. "La Naissance d'Une Danse Moderne en France." *Festival International de la Nouvelle Danse* souvenir catalog Montreal (1987).

——. "Quatre Siècles de Danse en France; La Suprematie Classique". *La Danse, la Naissance D'Un Mouvement de Pensée*. Val-de-Marne: Armand Collins, 1989. 25-31.

Newton, David. "Dance at Duke — What was America's avant-garde now one of France's newest Cultural Exports." *Daily News* Greensboro, NC (1983).

Novack, Cynthia. *Sharing the Dance: Contact Improvisation and American Culture*. Madison: U of Wisconsin P, 1990.

Noverre, Jean Georges. *Letters on Dancing and Ballet*. Trans. Cyril W. Beaumont. Brooklyn, NY: Dance Horizons, 1966.

Pally, Marcia. "The Rediscovery of Narrative: Dance in the 1980's." *Next Wave Festival* souvenir book (1984): 11-15.

Rainer, Yvonne. "Some Retrospective Notes on a Dance for 10 People and 12 Mattresses Called 'Parts of the Same Sextets', Performed at the Wadsworth Atheneum, Hartford, Connecticut, and Judson Memorial Church, New York in March 1965." *TDR* 30 (Winter 1965): 168.

Rich, Allan. "Stretching the Boundaries/Pina Bausch." *Newsweek* 18 June 1984.

Robertson, Allen. "Danse Nouvelle — A Modern Dance Boom Has Been Sweeping Away France The Past Few Years." *Ballet News* 5 (July 1983): 14-16.

——. "New French Dance." *TDR* 110 (Spring 1984): 103-109.

Roslavleva, Natalia. *Era of the Russian Ballet*. New York: DaCapo, 1979.

Searle, Humphrey. *Ballet Music*. New York: Dover, 1958.

Servos, Norbert. *Pina Baush — Wuppertal Dance Theater or the Art of Training a Goldfish*. Trans. Patricia Stadie. Cologne: Ballett-Buhnen-Verlag, 1984.

Siegel, Marcia. *The Shapes of Change — Images of American Dance*. Berkeley, Los Angeles, London: U of Califorina P, 1985.

——. "Expressionism and Dance." Seminar Department of Performance Studies, Tisch School of the Arts, New York University, Fall 1988.

Sirvin, Rene. "Stupefiant — Cendrillon de Maguy Marin." *L'Aurore* 2 December 1985.

Stewart, Virginia and Merle Armitage, eds. "The Modern Dance in Germany." *Modern Dance.* New York: Dance Horizons, 1970. 3-42.

Supree, Burt. "Freedom in Limits." *The Village Voice,* 27 Jan. 1987.

Terry, Walter. *Ballet Guide.* New York: Dodd, 1976.

Tobias, Tobi. Television Interview on Kurt Jooss. New York: PBS, 1976.

Verdussen, Monique. "Le Cendrillon de Maguy Marin." *Libre Belgique* 26 Feb. 1985.

Wigman, Mary. *The Language of Dance.* transl. Walter Sorell. Middletown, Conn:. Wesleyan UP, 1966.

Wiley, Roland John. *Tchaicovsky's Ballets.* Oxford (Oxford-shine): Claredon P; New York: Oxford UP, 1985.

Theoretical Framework

Ariés, Philippe. *Centuries of Childhood — A Social History of Family Life.* New York: Knopf, 1962.

Barthes, Roland. *Mythologies.* Trans. Annette Lavers. London: Granada, 1973.

——. *Image — Music — Text.* Trans. Stephen Heath. New York: Hill and Wang, 1977.

Baudrillard, Jean. *Les Stratégies Fatales.* Paris: Grasset, 1983.

Benjamin, Walter. "The Storyteller." *Illuminations, ed.* Hannah Arendt. New York: Schocken, 1983: 109.

Benvenuto, Bice and Roger Kennedy. *The Works of Jacques Lacan: An Introduction.* London: Free Association, 1986.

Bloch, Ernst. *The Utopian Function of Art and Literature*. Trans. Jack Zipes and Frank Mecklenburg. Cambridge: MIT P, 1987.

Brecht, Bertold. "On Allienation Effects in Chinese Acting." *Brecht on Theater ed.* John Willet. New York: Hill and Wang, 1982.

——. "Popularity and Realism." *Modern Art and Modernism: A Critical Anthology*, eds. Francis Franscina and Charles Harrison. New York: Harper and Row, 1967.

Derrida, Jacques. *Of Gramatology* Trans. Gayatri Chakravorty. Baltimore: Johns Hopkins UP, 1976.

Dube, Wolf-Dieter. *Expressionism*. London: Praeguer, 1972.

Eagleton, Terry. *The Ideology of the Aesthetic*. Oxford and Cambridge, MA: Basil Blackwell, 1990.

Fleming, William. *Arts & Ideas*. New York, Chicago, San Francisco: Holt, Rinehart, Winston, 1980.

Foster, Hal. *Recodings — Art, Spectacle, Cultural Politics*. Seattle, Washington: Bay, 1985.

Foucault, Michel. *The History of Sexuality*. New York: Pantheon, 1978.

Garraty, John A. and Peter Gay. *The Columbia History of the World*. New York: Harper & Row, 1972.

Jameson, Fredric. *The Political Uncounscious — Narrative as a Socially Symbolic Act*. Ithaca, NY: Cornell UP, 1981.

——. "Postmodernism and Consumer Society." *The Anti-Aesthetic*. Ed. Hal Foster. Port Townsend, Washington: Bay, 1983. 111-125.

Jencks, Charles. *Post-Modernism — The New Classicism in Art and Architecture*. New York: Rizzoli, 1987.

Krauss, Rosalind E. *The Originality of the Avant-Garde and the Other Modernist Myths.* Cambridge, MA: MIT P, 1985.

Luyten, Joseph M. *O Que E Literatura Popular.* Sao Paulo: Brasiliense, 1983.

Machlis, Joseph. *Enjoyment of Music.* New York: Norton, 1963.

Merleau-Ponty, Maurice. *Phenomenology of Perception.* New York: Humanities P, 1962.

Nietzsche, Friedrich Wilheim. *A Nietzsche Reader.* Introduction by R. J. Hollingdale. Harmondsworth, New York: Penguin, 1977.

Owens, Craig. "The Allegorical Impulse—Toward a Theory of Postmodernism.". *Art After Modernism: Rethinking Representation.* New York: The New Museum, 1984. 203-235.

Perrone-Moysés, Leyla. *Roland Barthes.* Sao Paulo: Brasiliense, 1983.

Raeff, Marc. *Understanding Imperial Russia.* New York: Columbia UP, 1984.

Rosenberg, Harold. *The Tradition of the New.* Chicago: U of Chicago P, 1982.

Sarup, Madan. *Post-Structuralism and Postmodernism—An Introduction.* Athens: U of Georgia P, 1989.

Sassure, Ferdinand de. *Course in General Linguistics.* London: Fontana, Collins, 1974.

Stewart, Susan. *On Longing: Narrative, Miniature, the Gigantic, the Souvenir, the Collection.* Baltimore: John Hopkins UP, 1984.

Sontag, Susan. *Against Interpretation.* New York: Farrar, 1966.

Trachtenberg, Stanley. "Introduction." *The Postmodern Moment—A Handbook of Contemporary Innovation in the Arts.* Westport, CT: Greenwood, 1985. 3-17.

Wallis, Brian, ed. "Introduction." *Art After Modernism: Rethinking Representation.* New York: The New Museum, 1984.

West, Cornel. Lecture. School of Education, Health, Nursing and Arts Professions, New York University, 12 March 1992.

Fairy Tales and Literature

Aarne, Antti. *The Types of the Folktales: A Classification and Bibliography.* Rev. and enlarged Stith Thompson. 2nd rev. ed. FF Communications Nr. 3. Helsinki: Suomalainen Tiedeakatemia, 1961.

Afanasev, Aleksandr. *Russian Fairy Tales.* New York: Pantheon, 1945.

Barchilon, Jacques. *Le Conte Merveilleux Français de 1690 a 1790.* Paris: Champion, 1975.

——. and Peter Flinders. *Charles Perrault.* Boston: Twayne, 1981.

Bausinger, Hermann. "Concerning the Content and Meaning of Fairy Tales." *The Germanic Review* 42 (Spring 1987): 75-82.

Bettelheim, Bruno. *The Uses of Enchantment: the Meaning and Importance of Fairy Tales.* New York: Random, 1975.

Bottingheimer, Ruth B, ed. "Silenced Women in the Grimms' Tales: The "Fit" Between Fairy Tale and Society in Their Historical Context." *Fairy Tales and Society: Illusion, Allusion and Paradigm.* Philadelphia: U of Pennsylvania P, 1986. 115-133.

——. *Grimm's Bad Girls and Bold Boys — The Moral & Social Vision of the Tales.* New Haven and London: Yale UP, 1987.

Calvino, Italo. ed. *Italian Folktales.* Trans. George Martin. New York: Pantheon, 1980.

Campbell, Joseph, ed. *The Complete Grimm's Fairy Tales.* New York: Pantheon, 1972.

——. *The Hero With a Thousand Faces.* Cleveland: Meridian, 1956.

Carter, Angela. *The Bloody Chamber.* New York: Harper and Row, 1979.

Collier, Mary Jeffrey. "The Psychological Appeal in the Cinderella Theme." *American Imago* 18 (1961): 399-406.

Dégh, Linda. *Folktales and Society: Storytelling in a Hungarian Peasant Community.* Trans. Emily Schlossberg. Bloomington: Indiana UP, 1969.

——. "Folk Narrative." *Folklore and Folklife.* Ed. Richard M. Dorson. Chicago: Chigago UP, 1972. 48:53.

——. *Studies in Eastern European Folk Narrative.* Bloomington: Indiana UP, 1978.

——. "Grimms' Household Tales and Its Place in the Household: The Social Relevance of a Controversial Classic." *Western Folklore* 38 (1979): 83-103.

——. "Magic For Sale: Märchen and Legend in TV Advertising." *Fabula* 20 (1979): 47-68.

Darnton, Robert. *The Great Cat Massacre and Other Episodes in French Cultural History.* New York: Basic, 1984.

Dundes, Alan. "Introduction to the Second Edition." *Morphology of the Folktale.* Vladimir Propp. Austin: U of Textas P, 1968.

——. *Cinderella: A Casebook.* New York: Garland, 1982.

——. "Fairy tales from a Folklorist Perspective." *Fairy Tales and Society — Illusion, Allusion and Paradigm.* Ed. Ruth Bottigheimer. Philadelphia: U of Pennsylvania P, 1986. 259-269.

——. "The Psychoanalytic Study of the Grimms' Tales with Special Reference to 'The Maiden Without Hands'." *The Germanic Review* 42 (Spring 1987): 50-63.

——, ed. *Little Red Ridding Hood*. Madison, WI: U of Wisconsin P, 1989.

Ellis, John. *One Fairy Story Too Many: The Brothers Grimm and Their Tales*. Chicago: U of Chicago P, 1983.

Franz, Marie-Louise von. *An Introduction to the Interpretation of the Fairy Tales*. New York: Spring, 1970.

——. *Problems of the Feminine in Fairy tales*. New York: Spring, 1972.

Grimm, Jacob and Wilheim. *German Fairy Tales—J. and W. Grimm and Others*. Eds. Helmut Bracket and Volkmar Sander. New York: The German Library, 1985.

Henriot, Emile, ed. *Contes de Perrault en Vers et en Prose*. Paris: Chronique des Lettres Françaises, 1928.

Jung, C.G. *Psyché and Symbol*. New York: Doubleday, 1958.

——. *Man and His Symbols*. New York: Dell, 1968.

Lang, Andrew, ed. *The Blue Fairy Tale Book*. New York: Dover, 1965.

Lee, Tanith. *Red as Blood*. New York: Daw, 1983.

Lieberman, Marcia. "Some Day My Prince Will Come: Female Acculturation Through the Fairy Tales." *College English* 34 (1972): 383-95.

Luthi, Max. *The Fairytales as An Art Form and Portrait of Man*. Trans. John Erickson. Bloomington: Indiana UP, 1987.

Minard, Rosemary. *Womenfolk and Fairy Tales*. Boston: Houghton Mifflin, 1975.

Morgan Zarucchi, Jeanne, ed. *Charles Perrault: memories of My Life*. Columbia: U of Missouri P, 1989.

Mourney, Lilyane. *Introduction aux contes de Grimm et de Perrault*. Paris: Minard, 1978.

Opie, Iona and Peter. *The Classic Fairy Tales*. London, New York, Toronto: Oxford UP, 1974.

Perrault, Charles. *The Fairy Tales of Charles Perrault*. Trans. Angela Carter. New York: Avon, 1977.

Philip, Neil. *The Cinderella Story*. London: Penguin Books, 1989.

Propp, Vladimir. *Morphlogy of the Folktale*. Eds. Louis Wagner and Alan Dundes. Trans. Laurence Scott. 2nd rev. ed. Austin: U of Texas P, 1968.

——. "Les Transformations des Contes Fantastiques." *Théorie de la Literature*. Trans. and Ed. Tzvetan Todorov. Paris: 1965: 234-261.

Robert, Raymonde. *Le Conte des fées literaires en France de la fin du XVIIè a la fin du XVIIè siècle*. Nancy: Presses Universitaires de Nancy, 1982.

Rojcewicz, Peter M. "Retellings: The Nursery and Household Tales of the Brothers Grimm.".*On The Next Wave* Brooklyn: Brooklyn Academy of Music (1989): 8-13.

Rouger, Gilbert. *Contes de Perrault*. Paris: Garnier, 1967.

Rowe, Karen E. "To Spin a Yarn: The Female Voice in Folklore and Fairy Tales." *Fairy Tales and Society—Illusion, Allusion and Paradigm*. Ed. Ruth Bottingheimer. Philadelphia: U of Pennsylvania P, 1986. 53-75.

Schenda, Rudolf. "Telling Tales—Spreading Tales: Change in the Communicative Forms of a Popular Genre." *Fairy Tales and Society—Illusion, Allusion and Paradigm*. Ed. Ruth

Bottigheimer. Philadelphia: U of Pennsylvania P, 1986. 75-95.

Sexton, Anne. *The Complete Poems*. Boston: Houghton Mifflin, 1981. ed. Maxine Kumin.

Stone, Kay "Things Walt Disney Never Told Us." *Women and Folklore*. Ed. Claire R. Farrer. Austin and London: U of Texas P, 1975. 42-50.

——. "The Misuses of Enchantment: Controversies on the Significance of Fairy Tales." *Women's Folklore, Women's Culture*. Eds. Rosan A. Jordan and Susan J. Kalcik. Philadelphia: U of Pennsylvania P, 1985.

——. "Feminist Approaches to the Interpretation of Fairy Tales." *Fairy Tales and Society—Illusion, Allusion and Paradigm*. Ed. Ruth Bottigheimer. Philadelphia: U of Pennsylvania P, 1986. 229-237.

Tatar, Maria M. "Born Yesterday: Heroes in the Grimm's Fairy Tales." *Fairy Tales and Society—Illusion, Allusion and Paradigm*. Ed. Ruth Bottigheimer. Philadelphia: U of Pennsylvania P, 1986. 95-115.

Thompson, Stith. *The Folktale*. New York: Dryen, 1946.

Weber, Eugen. "Fairies and Hard Facts: the realities of folktales." *Journal of the History of Ideas*. XLII (1981): 93-113.

Zipes, Jack. *Breaking the Magic Spell—Radical Theories of Folk and Fairy Tales*. Austin: U of Texas P, 1979.

——. *Fairy Tales and The Art of Subversion*. New York: Methuen, 1983.

——, ed. *Don't Bet on the Prince*. New York: Methuen, 1986.

——. *The Brothers Grimm—From Enchanted Forests to the Modern World*. Routledge, New York and London: Routledge, 1988.

——. *Beauties, Beasts and Enchantments — Classic French Fairy Tales*. New York: Meridian, 1991.

Videotapes

Bluebeard. Recorded in Wuppertal, for the Tanztheater Wuppertal. Distribution by Editions Arche, Paris, 1989 [1977], VHS, color, 110 minutes.

Cinderella. Recorded in Lyon for the Lyon Opera Ballet. Courtesy Antoine Manologlou, Companie Maguy Marin. Creteil, 1990 [1985], VHS, color, 100 minutes.

The Handless Maiden. Recorded in New York city for the Home for Contemporary Theater, 1987. VHS, color, 35 minutes.

A Primer for Pina. Presented by Susan Sontag. Recorded in London, Channel 4, by City Documentaries Producers, 1984. Aired on PBS, New York, 1986. VHS, color, 35 minutes.

Sleeping Beauty. Recorded in Saint Petersburg (then Leningrad) with the Kirov Ballet. Distribution in the United States by Thorn EMI Videos, 1983. VHS, color, 148 minutes.

Interviews

Kotoske, Tamar, Maria Lakis and Mary Ritcher. Personal Interview. New York, 17 May 1988.

Kotoske, Tamar. Telephone Interview. New York, 5 Aug. 1989.

Marin, Maguy. Personal Interview. Paris, 21 June 1990.

Bausch, Pina. Personal Interview. New York, 19 November 1991.

Appendix

A Summary of Propp's Diagram Used in the Book for a Morphological Analysis of Fairy Tales

(α)	Initial situation
(a)	A lack
(A)	Villainy
(A^6)	Villainy--Mutilation
(A^{11})	Villainy--The casting of a spell
(A^{13})	Villainy--Order to kill
(A^{17})	Villainy--Cannibalism
(B^5)	Mediation
(L)	Claims of a false hero
(μ^3)	Coersion/deception
(λ)	Preliminary Misfortune
(δ^1)	Order violated
(δ^2)	Order carried on
(γ')	Interdiciton
(φ^2)	The hero receives information about the villain
(E^3)	Reconnaissance by others to obtain information about the villain
(θ^2)	The hero falls victim of a magical agent
($D^{5/7}$)	Request for Mercy and other request
(H)	New struggle with the villain
(C)	Consent to Counteraction
(B^5)	Mediation
($\uparrow$)	Departure
(G)	Transference of the hero to a designated place
(G^3)	The Hero is led to a designated place
(H^2)	The place of confrontation with the villain

(o)	*Unrecognized arrival*
(P)	*Pursuit of the hero*
(B^1)	*Call for help*
(B^7)	*Lament or cry for help*
(F)	*Receipt of magical help*
(F^5)	*Agent/helper is found*
(F^6)	*The helper*
($F^{6/9}$)	*The meeting with a magical helper*
(F^9)	*Agent/helper offers services*
(F)	*Receipt of magical help*
(D^1)	*The helper's tasks for the hero*
(D^2)	*The hero is interrogated*
(J^2)	*Transference of a lost object*
(L)	*Claims of false heroes*
(Q)	*Recognition of the hero*
(I)	*Victory over the villain*
(I^1)	*Victory over the villain in open battle*
(I^2)	*Victory without battle*
(U)	*Punishment of the villain*
(U^-)	*Villains are not punished*
(K)	*Liquidation of initial misfortune*
(K^4)	*Liquidation of misfortune as a direct result from previous action*
(K^9)	*Ressucitation*
(W)	*Wedding*
(W^*)	*Wedding and accession to the throne*
(W^o)	*Monetary reward*
(+)	*Positive result*
(-)	*Negative result*

NEW CONNECTIONS
Studies in Interdisciplinarity

This series has as its focus the interrelationships between literature and the other arts, science, philosophy, law, psychology, anthropology, and religion. Book-length manuscripts of at least 200 pages examining and illustrating the intricacies of these interrelationships will be considered. Comparative studies emphasizing new methods of dealing with critical or theoretical problems between disciplines will be given preference. Consideration will also be given to studies of other humanities disciplines engaged in interdisciplinary dialogues.

The series editor is: Shirley Paolini
Dean, School of Human Sciences and Humanities
University of Houston, Clear Lake
2700 Bay Area Blvd.
Houston, TX 77058